Applied Business

GCSE

Richard Barrett

Published in 2002 by:

Nelson Thornes Ltd
Delta Place
27 Bath Road
CHELTENHAM
GL53 7TH
United Kingdom

03 04 05 06 / 10 9 8 7 6 5 4 3

A catalogue record for this book is available from the British Library

ISBN 0 7487 5745 7

Illustrations by Woody Fox

Page make-up by Multiplex Techniques Ltd

Printed and bound in Spain by Graphicas Estella

UNIT 1
Investigating Business

UNIT 2
People and Business

UNIT 3
Business Finance

Introduction

This book is written to help students and teachers preparing for the GCSE course in Applied Business. Its contents will also find a place in a number of other introductory business programmes. The book aims to steer away from an academic, theoretical discussion of business. With regular reference to household names, I have tried to use as many real business situations and examples as possible to demonstrate how business operates in a practical way. I have also tried to highlight some of the skills and attitudes young people will need to succeed in the world of work.

The sections of the book match the units of the GCSE in Applied Business (Double Award). The contents are intended to assist students in putting together their assessed work and in preparing for the external assessment. In order to do this, there are several sections within each unit. The 'Jargon dragon' explains unfamiliar words as they occur and there is a glossary of terms at the end of the book. The 'Find it Out' feature suggests activities for obtaining more information and the various web sites detailed in the text are a useful starting point for this research. 'Think it Through' is an opportunity for students to discuss some business issues for which there is rarely a right or wrong answer, but the feature encourages the use of analysis and discussion. The case studies are short, usually real-life, examples of what has happened in businesses and are accompanied by short questions to reinforce learning and understanding. Readers who require more material to work with should take advantage of the web and print-based materials written specifically to support this book. Details are available from the publisher at www.nelsonthornes.com or by calling 01242 267270.

I would like to thank Evelyn Wheeler, Mike Chappell, Glynis Frater and Paula Miles for their help in commenting on the early drafts of this text. Jane, Claire, Fiona and Rick at Nelson Thornes were, as ever, patient and helpful during the process of developing the book, and I am once again grateful to them. Big thanks to Marie, Michelle and James for putting up with their absent husband and father as the book entered its final stages of preparation.

Richard Barrett
November 2001

How this book is organised

Units   Each unit covers all the information and underpinning you will need for this section of the specification.

Unit Introduction   Each unit has an introduction that will give you an overview of what is covered in that unit.

Jargon Dragon   Jargon dragons define important terms and words that you may be unfamiliar with.

Find It Out   This feature is used to suggest ways in which you can carry out your own research and investigation.

Think It Through   This feature is designed to develop your research and investigation skills further, to allow you to gain high grades. Using these features will also help you to develop your analytical, discussion and evaluation skills.

Case Studies   The case studies in each chapter outline real situations from the world of business. Working on the questions at the end of each case study will help you apply the theory you have learned to real business situations.

Glossary   The glossary at the end of the book contains all the words defined in the jargon dragons.

How your work will be assessed

Unit 1, *Investigating Business*, will be internally assessed by teachers at your school or college. You will be asked by your teachers to carry out assignments and projects as part of this unit.

Unit 2, *People and Business*, will also be internally assessed by teachers at your school or college. Again, you will be asked by your teachers to carry out assignments and projects for this unit.

Unit 3, *Business Finance*, will be assessed by an external examination.

Internal assessment

The internal assessments of Units 1 and 2 are through written assignments and projects that will be set by your teachers.

I hope you will find this book useful for your course. Good luck!

Richard Barrett

Acknowledgements

The author and publisher would like to thank the following people and organisations for permission to reproduce material in this book:

Images:
B. Apicella/Photofusion for part of the image on pages 2/3; The Authentic Bread Company for information for the image on page 109; Basic Skills for the photo on page 150; Boots plc for the photos on pages 41 and 164; BP plc for the logos on page 153; Bureau Veritas Quality International and the United Kingdom Accreditation Service for the logo on page 32; Consignia plc for the logo on page 8; Corbis Images for the photos on pages 65, 70, 100 and 104; Corel (NT) for part of the images on pages 2/3 and 175; Crown Copyright for the form on page 82 and the screenshot on page 102; The Department of Trade and Industry for the map on page 12; Derby Citizens' Advice Bureau for the photo on page 132; Digital Stock (NT) for the photo on page 99; Digital Vision (NT) for the photo on page 88; Dixons Group plc for the balance sheet on page 170 and the profit and loss account on page 182; Dunlop Slazenger for the photo on page 30; Elektravision (NT) for the photo on page 155; Getty Images for the photos on pages 144 and 154; GUS Home Shopping Ltd for the image on page 133; Investors in People UK for the logo on page 121; M. Sookias/NT for the photo on page 146; National Association of Citizens' Advice Bureaux for the logo and photo on page 132; National Coaches for the photo on page 178; National Westminster Bank plc for the image on page 35; Neill Bruce's Automobile Photo Library for the photo on page 152; Photodisc (NT) for the photos on pages 27, 59, 61, 62/63, 65, 84, 104, 111, 129, 134/35 and part of the image on page 175; Photofusion for the photos on pages 7, 15, 23, 34, 44, 52, 69, 79, and 119; Rubberball (NT) for the photo on page 6; Stockbyte (NT) for the photo on page 66; Tesco Ltd for the photos on pages 37 and 39; Tupperware UK and Ireland for the image on page 80; and Andrew Wiard/reportphotos.com for the photo on page 89.

Text:
The Association of Accounting Technicians (AAT) for information in the case study on pages 158/59; The Authentic Bread Company Ltd for information for the image on page 109; Companies House for information in the case study on pages 172/73; The Confederation of British Industry (CBI) for information in the case study on page 67; The Department of

Trade and Industry for information in the case study on pages 176/77; The Guardian for information in the case study on pages 52/53; Insignia World Office Rents for information in the case study on page 9; The Trades Union Congress (TUC) for information in the case study on pages 92/93; Vodafone Ltd for information in the case study on page 59; and The Yorkshire Evening Post for information in the case study on pages 104/05.

We would also like to thank Mike Chappell, Glynis Frater, Paula Miles, Dave Needham and Evelyn Wheeler for their help in reviewing the manuscript for this book.

We have made every effort to contact copyright holders and apologise if anyone has been overlooked.

Dedication

This book is dedicated to the memory of Alice Barrett.

What's in this unit?

This unit tells you about the aims and objectives businesses set for themselves and why they set them. You will learn about the different types of business ownership and how this makes a difference to business activity. There are different sorts of business activity and different businesses organise themselves differently to carry out their tasks. Communication between the various parts of a business is important.

Before they can start providing goods or services, businesses have to choose their location and consider how they will use technology in their activities. This unit helps you to understand how they do this, as well as some of the influences on business activity. We will look at how businesses can affect the wider community, in particular what has to be done by businesses to reduce any harm to the environment that their activities might cause.

This unit will help you to prepare for your assessment, which requires you to investigate two contrasting businesses in detail. After working through it, you should have a better understanding of the ownership of the two businesses and how they relate to the wider business world.

Investigating Business 1

In this unit you will learn about:

Aims and objectives

Successful businesses know clearly what they want to do and how they want to do it. In business jargon this means that they have clear **aims**. The aims of businesses can include:

- making a profit
- providing goods or services
- surviving as a business
- expanding the business
- maximising sales
- improving product quality
- providing a competitive service
- providing charitable or voluntary services
- being environmentally friendly.

Objectives are the targets the business will set itself so it can check that it is making progress to achieving its aims.

Objectives are the steps towards achieving business aims

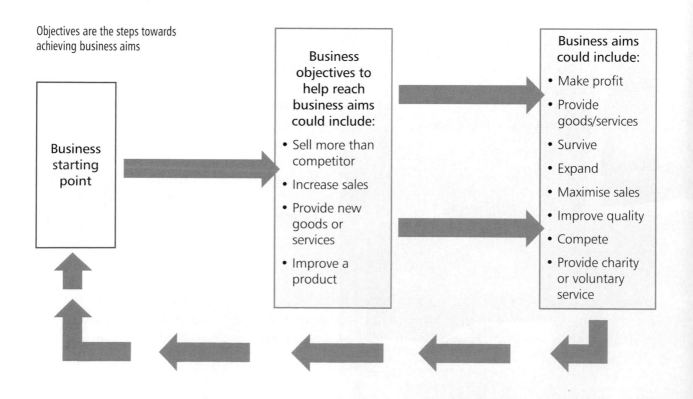

Business starting point

Business objectives to help reach business aims could include:

- Sell more than competitor
- Increase sales
- Provide new goods or services
- Improve a product

Business aims could include:

- Make profit
- Provide goods/services
- Survive
- Expand
- Maximise sales
- Improve quality
- Compete
- Provide charity or voluntary service

Objectives can include:

- selling more of a product than a competitor
- providing more goods or services than in the previous year
- providing new goods or services
- improving a product.

THE JARGON DRAGON

maximise sales – sell as many as possible

For example, if a business decided that its aim is to <u>maximise sales</u> it might set itself the objectives of selling 10% more than in the previous year and of being at least halfway to this aim by the middle of the year. It would then organise its production and sales activity to ensure the aim and objectives were met. Managers could check sales figures during the year to ensure that progress is being made. If production was too low it could be increased. If sales were not high enough more sales staff could be employed or existing staff trained to be better. This shows how the aims and objectives of an organisation affect its activity.

Objectives are normally measurable and are set to be achieved within a certain time. It is common for the different parts of a business to have different aims and objectives. These are designed to support the overall aims and objectives of the business. Businesses may publish their aims and objectives on their annual reports, on their website or in publicity material.

Look at some business reports and publications and describe the aims and objectives they have set themselves. A number are listed at this address:
`www.bized.ac.uk/listserv/companies/`
`comlist.htm`

FIND IT OUT

Business ownership

There are different sorts of business ownership. Each type has different advantages and disadvantages to the owners. The type of ownership may change as a business grows and develops. When you investigate businesses for your assessment you will need to explain what sort of ownership they have and why.

The main types of business ownership

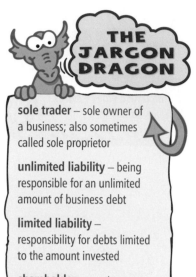

THE JARGON DRAGON

sole trader – sole owner of a business; also sometimes called sole proprietor

unlimited liability – being responsible for an unlimited amount of business debt

limited liability – responsibility for debts limited to the amount invested

shareholders – part owners of a company

Sole owner

Some businesses are owned by only one person (usually very small businesses, such as a shop, painter and decorator, hairdresser or mobile disco). Sole owners can employ people to work for them and some can grow to be quite large. Sole owners are sometimes called **sole traders** or **sole proprietors**. The sole trader can give personal attention to customers and anyone who works for him or her. The amount the owner can spend on equipment and materials when starting the business is restricted to how much he or she can borrow or save. The sole trader is her or his own boss and can make quick decisions without having to get someone else's agreement. The owner is responsible, or liable, for all debts and actions of the business. This means that if the business fails they might have to sell their personal possessions to repay the debts. This is known as **unlimited liability**.

Partnership

A partnership is a group of two or more people who set up a business together. Doctors, solicitors and dentists usually work in partnerships. The sort of businesses carried out by sole traders can also be carried out by partnerships. Partnerships can normally raise more money than sole traders and are able to share work but the partners may disagree about how to run the business. Most partnerships have unlimited liability, just like the sole trader. Occasionally a limited partnership may be established. This means that partners who have no active part in running the business, who are known as 'sleeping partners', can have **limited liability**. The active partners will still have unlimited liability.

There are many different types of sole trader

Private limited company

This is a larger sort of business. You can tell when a business is a private company because it has to have Limited or Ltd after its name. This warns anyone doing business with the firm that the owners have limited liability. In other words, if the business fails the owners – the **shareholders** – will lose only what they have already invested and are not personally liable in the way that sole owners or most partnerships are. Private companies are involved in different sorts of business, from engineering to large retail chain stores. Private companies can raise much more money than a sole owner or a partnership. The size of these companies means that sometimes the owners lose their personal touch with their employees or customers.

Public limited company

You can tell a public company because it has to have PLC after its name (PLC stands for Public Limited Company). This is the largest sort of business and is allowed to invite members of the public to become shareholders. The shareholders have limited liability.

Public companies are very large. Most supermarkets are public companies. Banks and large chemical and engineering businesses have this sort of ownership. Public companies are able to afford to employ experts and so become very profitable. One criticism of PLCs is that they are too large and the managers are out of touch with employees and customers.

Co-operative

In a co-operative organisation the people who work there are the owners. The Co-op is probably the most well known co-operative. Its stores are owned by shoppers and employees. Agricultural co-operatives are also common as a way for farmers to share expenses and equipment. Co-operatives try to run on democratic principles and often support worthwhile social aims as well as aiming to make profits for the owners. Social aims can include supporting a local brass band or providing education classes for members.

Franchise

A franchise is an agreement that allows one business to copy the successful methods and organisation of another business. Although all the businesses might look the same, each branch is, in fact, owned by different people – usually sole owners or partnerships. Fast food shops like MacDonald's and high-street

THE JARGON DRAGON

democratic – method of organisation where members have a say in how things are organised. This is usually done through members voting for elected representatives to put forward their views.

franchise – an agreement for one business to copy the successful organisation of another

MacDonald's is a well-known franchise

franchisee – someone who buys a franchise

franchisor – the firm that sells the franchise business to the franchisee

council tax – household tax paid to local council, based on the value of your house

printers such as KallKwik are often organised as franchises. The franchisee has the advantage of knowing they are using an already successful approach and a name customers will recognise. They may have to pay a regular part of their earnings to the franchisor. Franchisees are restricted by the franchisor on how they can develop their business.

Public sector businesses

All of the businesses mentioned so far are known as private sector businesses. This is because private individuals or groups of private individuals own them. Businesses owned by local or national government on behalf of the public are in the public sector. Local government (the councils which run your town, county, city or village) often provide services such as sports centres or swimming pools for local people to use. These facilities are organised by paid employees of the council.

Councils receive their money from the public who pay to use their facilities, from the government and from the **council tax** payments each household has to make. People who run councils – the councillors – are elected by the public. Councillors are unpaid, but may claim expenses for this voluntary work, which they do alongside their usual job. Paid officials make sure the business activities are run to the satisfaction of the councillors and the public.

Public corporations usually have a well-known logo (Royal Mail and the Royal Mail cruciform are registered trademarks of Consignia plc)

Different types of business provide the goods and services we need

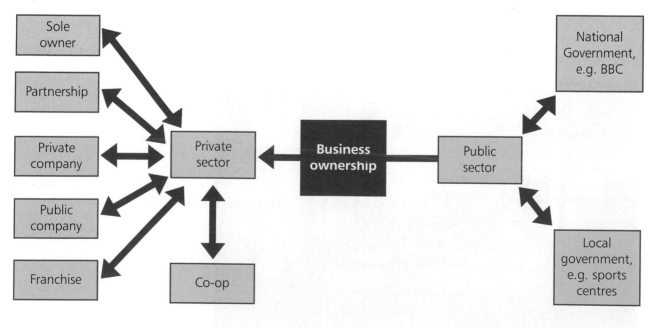

National government controls public corporations (not to be confused with public *companies*, which are in the private sector), which operate on a national scale for the benefit of the public. Paid officials, who are responsible to a government minister and Parliament, carry out the work of public corporations. The best known public corporation is the BBC. Since the 1980s, the government has sold off shares in public corporations to make them public companies in the belief that they will be run more efficiently. This is known as privatisation. British Telecom was previously a public corporation, and the rail service was also run as a public corporation known as British Rail, rather than as a collection of separate companies as it is now.

Business location

Where a business chooses to place itself, or locate, is an important consideration.

You need to understand what influenced the businesses you study to locate themselves where they are now. There are many factors the businesses would have considered:

The number of people available with suitable skills

Certain areas of the country are linked to certain types of industry. For example, English pottery making is centred around Stoke on Trent in Staffordshire. Businesses looking to start or expand pottery making know that if they locate in that area they are more likely to be able to find staff trained with the skills they need. This saves money by reducing costs of training.

The cost of labour

Wages tend to be higher in certain parts of the country where the cost of living is high – for example, in London and the south-east of England. Firms that want to keep labour costs low will tend to go to areas where wages are generally lower or where there are large numbers of unemployed people willing to take

retail – shop open to the public

business rates – tax businesses pay to local council based on the estimated rental value of the business' premises

assisted area – part of the country where an enterprise grant is available to small businesses

lower paid work rather than live on benefits. This is one of the reasons why a number of call centres have been established in the north-east of England – the area tends to have higher levels of unemployment than the rest of the country.

The cost of premises

Premises costs tend to be higher in the south-east of England than elsewhere. Around the country **retail** premises will cost more in city centres or major shopping centres, such as the Trafford Centre. Costs will be lower in outlying shopping areas around a town or city. Retail or office premises that are on the ground floor of a high street will be more expensive than those above street level or located away from the high street. The cost of industrial or warehouse premises will be affected by how close the premises are to major motorway and rail networks.

Look in a local newspaper or estate agents to find the price of shop premises. Do the prices change according to the area where the premises are? Why do you think this is the case?

Local government charges

The households in an area pay council tax, businesses have to pay **business rates**. These rates pay for things like waste disposal, street lighting and road maintenance. The level of business rates is linked to a property's rental value and will vary from council to council. It adds to the costs of running the business. Firms will consider the likely level of business rates when deciding where to locate.

Financial help

The government or the European Union (EU) may provide areas of high unemployment with financial help to develop business activity and employment. For example, an Enterprise Grant of up to £75 000 is available in certain parts of the country (**assisted areas**) to help small and medium-sized businesses purchase equipment or land. In some areas Regional Selective Assistance is available for projects that are worth more than £500 000.

City	Annual rent, as quoted locally
Manchester	£21.00 per sq ft
Dublin	€45.00 per sq ft
Glasgow	£22.00 per sq ft
Birmingham	£24.00 per sq ft
London City	£58.00 per sq ft

Based on www.manchestercalling.com/website/propertysites.
factsfigures.html. **Insignia World Office Rents 2001**

Q1 *Copy this information into a computer spreadsheet so you can sort the cities according to which is the most expensive.*

Q2 *If you were choosing to locate an office, which one of these cities would you choose?*

Q3 *What factors, apart from cost of office space, would you consider in deciding where to locate the office?*

Financial help from the government is managed by the Department of Trade and Industry (`www.dti.gov.uk`). Local councils can sometimes provide financial help for businesses in their areas.

The areas marked in blue on this map are areas where the Enterprise Grant may be paid to businesses

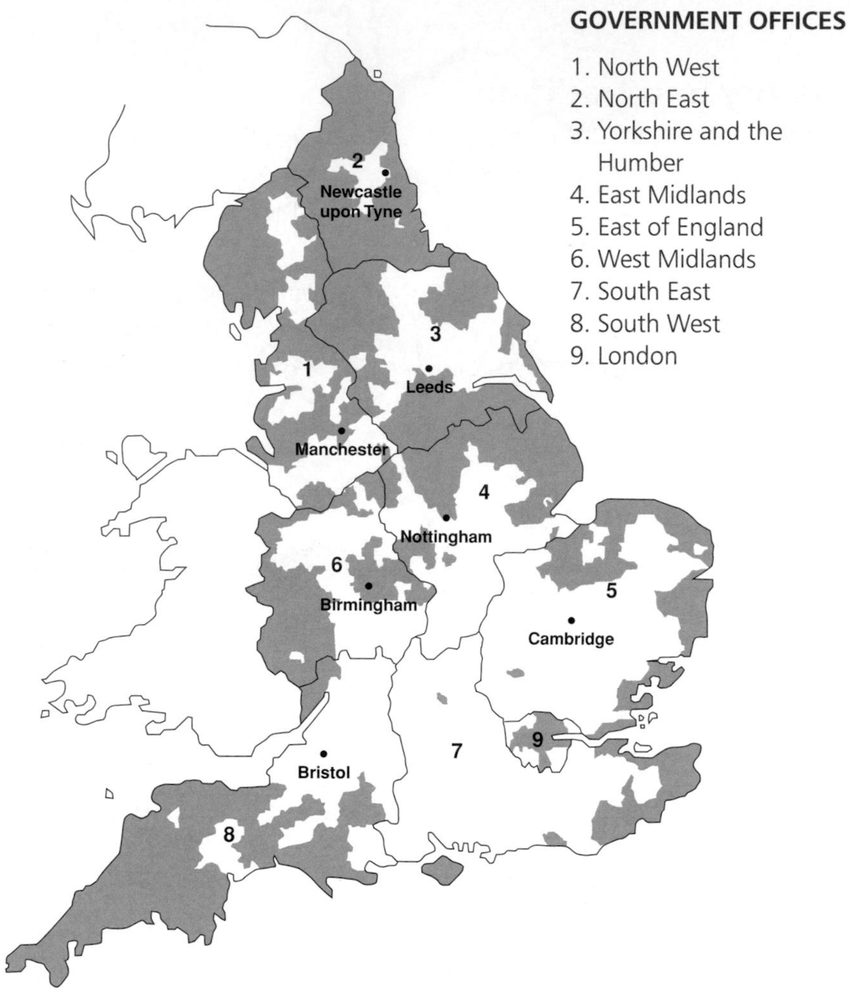
GOVERNMENT OFFICES
1. North West
2. North East
3. Yorkshire and the Humber
4. East Midlands
5. East of England
6. West Midlands
7. South East
8. South West
9. London
Newcastle upon Tyne
Leeds
Manchester
Nottingham
Birmingham
Cambridge
Bristol

Transport links for supplies and distribution

The location chosen by the business has to be accessible. Local customers need to be able to reach it easily. Businesses that distribute goods and services nationally or internationally need to be near suitable transport such as motorways, railways and airports.

The need to be where customers are

By being near its customers a firm has more chance of making sales. Being near customers also reduces transport costs. It is for this reason that larger breweries are still to be found in cities such as Manchester, Newcastle and London when similar-sized manufacturers of other products have moved outside the city. The beer and lager produced by the breweries is bulky and difficult to transport. City centre location of breweries, near to pubs and hotels, reduces the cost and time involved in moving the finished products to where they are needed.

History and tradition

In the past certain areas have been linked to certain products – for example, Sheffield to steel, Newcastle upon Tyne to shipbuilding, Stoke-on-Trent to pottery and High Wycombe to furniture. Originally there were sound commercial reasons for these businesses to locate where they did (for example, Sheffield had easy access to iron ore, transport and coal). As long as these advantages remain it is sensible for businesses to follow history and tradition. If these advantages are reduced, or become greater elsewhere, history and tradition will be less important and businesses may move away.

Stoke-on-Trent has long been known as 'The Potteries'

Sales techniques

Traditional retail activities need showrooms or shops for the public to visit and look at and try out the items for sale. Activities such as selling cars or clothes require space that is easily accessible. Selling over the Internet, by telephone or through mail order removes the need for special locations and gives the business more choice of where to be based.

Location decisions involve
considering many factors

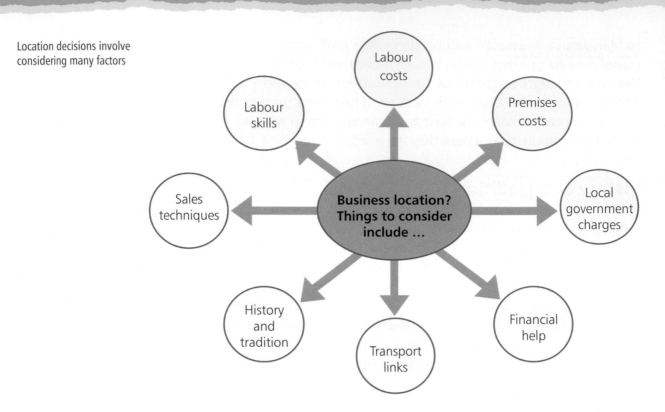

In practice no *one* consideration influences where a business will
locate. Owners and managers will carefully consider all the
matters mentioned here and come to a decision about what they
believe to be best. Your investigations should try to establish
some of the more important considerations made by the
business you investigate.

Business activity

THE JARGON DRAGON

goods – physical objects that
can be transferred to others

services – activities performed
by people for others that cannot
be transferred

Businesses carry out many activities. Some may produce **goods**,
for example furniture, clothes or computers. Others may produce
services such as web page design, car repair or hairdressing. You
need to be able to establish the main activities of the business
you investigate.

Business activities are analysed in the following groups by
government and economists:

- Manufacturing
- Sales
- Client services
- Other services.

Manufacturing

This could mean making **capital goods**. Kitchen equipment used in restaurants, drills used to make children's toys and lorries that carry out deliveries are all capital goods. Manufacturers also make **consumer goods**. These are goods sold to individuals for their own use at home or in their leisure time and not to make goods or services for others. Radios, televisions and sports equipment are examples of consumer goods.

Producing raw goods – raw goods are sometimes called **raw materials**. Businesses that produce raw goods extract them from the Earth. For this reason they are known as the *extractive* industries.

Consumer goods are all around us

Farmers producing wheat, milk and sheep in agriculture, trawler fishing, mining and forestry work that produces timber are examples of business activity producing raw goods.

Sales

This may be retail sales in shops or it could be **wholesale** (selling large quantities to shops from large warehouses). Mail order and Internet selling fall into the sales category.

Client services

Internet service providers such as AOL and Freeserve come into this category. Financial services such as insurance and banking, health care, dentistry and leisure and sport also provide client services.

Other services

This category covers things that do not fit into the other groups, such as transport and communications.

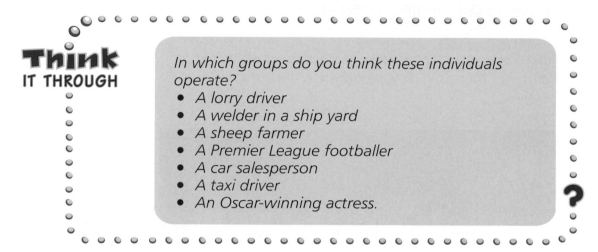

Think IT THROUGH

In which groups do you think these individuals operate?
- *A lorry driver*
- *A welder in a ship yard*
- *A sheep farmer*
- *A Premier League footballer*
- *A car salesperson*
- *A taxi driver*
- *An Oscar-winning actress.*

The case study on page 17 summarises the changes in employment in each of the above groups since the late 1970s.

Functional areas within business

THE JARGON DRAGON

business functions – tasks that have to be carried out by all businesses

Large businesses are split up into departments to carry out a range of tasks to support their activities. Small businesses may not have departments but they will still have to deal with the same sorts of tasks. These tasks, or **business functions** as they are called, can be summarised as:

- Human resources
- Finance
- Administration and IT support
- Operations
- Marketing and Sales
- Customer Service
- Research and Development.

Table A: Overall employment

	Total UK jobs	Agriculture, fishing and mining, etc	Manufacturing and construction	All services
1979	27 044	1337	8997	16 710
1981	25 978	1322	7954	16 702
1983	25 231	1251	7218	16 761
1985	26 226	1204	7234	17 788
1987	26 797	1110	7191	18 496
1989	28 631	1088	7695	19 848
1991	27 978	1042	6916	20 020
1993	26 897	914	6157	19 826
1995	27 363	814	6199	20 350
1997	28 194	821	6251	21 123
1999	28 870	729	6171	21 972
2001	29 229	689	5982	22 558

Table B: Employment in service industries

	Distribution, hotels and restaurants	Transport and communication	Banking, finance and insurance	Public administration, education, and health	Other services
1979	5500	1693	2850	5552	1115
1981	5465	1646	2919	5559	1113
1983	5426	1565	3066	5584	1120
1985	5776	1545	3400	5772	1296
1987	5812	1563	3677	6094	1351
1989	6355	1659	4190	6186	1458
1991	6299	1654	4310	6348	1409
1993	6179	1599	4299	6359	1389
1995	6306	1584	4565	6412	1484
1997	6501	1632	4963	6434	1592
1999	6680	1698	5332	6574	1688
2001	6824	1833	5485	6721	1695

Based on data from the Office of National Statistics
(http://www.statistics.gov.uk/statbase/timezone.asp)

Q1 *Using a spreadsheet or calculator work out the percentage change in the numbers employed in each type of job between 1979 and 2001 (Table A).*

Q2 *In what type of business activity has there been the greatest reduction in jobs?*

Q3 *What type of business activity has had the biggest growth in jobs?*

Q4 *Calculate the percentage of total jobs in each of Agriculture, Manufacturing and Services in 1979. How were these percentages different in 2001?*

Q5 *What type of service jobs have had the largest and smallest increases (Table B)?*

A person who owns their own business may have to deal with all of these tasks alone. Large businesses may have separate departments for each. When you investigate businesses you should find out how each of these tasks or functions is organised.

Human resources

A firm needs to be able to select the right people for the jobs it has and ensure that its employees – the people who work for the firm – work well and are content. The part of the business that deals with matters relating to the workforce might be called the Personnel Department, the Human Resource Department, the Manpower Section or the Staffing Department. Whatever name is used, the department needs to look after the business's staff or personnel needs. The Human Resource Department look after:

- recruitment, retention and dismissal of staff
- working conditions
- training, development and promotion
- employee organisations and unions
- health and safety.

Links to other departments

The Human Resources Department must link up with the other parts of the organisation to make sure that the right sort of personnel are being recruited and managed properly (see page 108). To carry out its work the Department must make sure it obeys employment law so members need to be able to draw on some legal skills. In order to ensure the workforce is working efficiently and effectively it also uses skills relating to psychology (how individuals think and act) and sociology (how individuals think and act in groups). To help employees work as effectively as possible their work and rewards need to be organised in a way that helps individuals to meet their own needs, as well as the needs of the firm. The Human Resources Department has an important role in helping to motivate or encourage employees to work to the best of their ability.

Successful businesses develop their goods and services to anticipate customers' demands and satisfy them. It is important that a firm's employees are kept up to date with changes and developments that affect their jobs and careers. This not only benefits the firm but also improves the employees' future job prospects.

The role of the Human Resources Department

The Human Resources Department is involved in the process of **staff development** as its work with the employee continues right up to when he or she leaves the firm. Page 117 gives more details about training and staff development.

THE JARGON DRAGON

staff development – training and helping staff to improve in their jobs

What are the advantages and disadvantages to an employer of training an employee?

Think IT THROUGH

Recruitment, retention and dismissal of staff

The swift pace of economic and technological change means that most people will change jobs several times in their life. There are four main reasons why a person might leave a job:

- Retirement
- Dismissal
- Redundancy
- Personal reasons

The Human Resources Department will be involved in all of these decisions.

Retirement

In most industries the retirement age is accepted as 65 years for men and 60 years for women, although many people work beyond these ages. Some people may also retire earlier than this.

THE JARGON DRAGON

dismissal – employee is required to leave their job

notice – agreed period of time an employee must work before leaving their job

payment in lieu of notice – employee is paid for the notice period but not required to work

misconduct – any behaviour that is disruptive or results in poor job performance

gross misconduct – dishonesty, theft, fighting and drunkenness, which may be grounds for immediate dismissal

Dismissal

An employee is **dismissed** or 'sacked' when they are told to leave their job. Usually he or she is given **notice** – allowed to work for a certain period of time before their employment ends. Sometimes dismissed employees are paid for the notice period but not required to work. This is called **payment in lieu of notice**. Employees will be dismissed with notice if they are capable of doing their job. Employees may be judged incapable of doing the job if their attendance is poor, if the work they do is not up to standard or if their attitude or behaviour is below the standards expected by the firm.

Employers must be able to give employees exact details of why they are considered unsuitable for the job. A clear job description is important in helping to do this and in avoiding misunderstandings. Advice and help to enable the employee to improve should also be provided, along with sufficient warnings about the situation. An employer who fails to provide these could face a claim for unfair dismissal. **Misconduct**, such as repeatedly failing to obey instructions, is another reason for dismissal. In rare cases an employee might be dismissed without notice. **Gross misconduct**, such as theft, fighting or drunkenness can lead to dismissal without notice.

Fighting and drunkenness can lead to dismissal without notice

Constructive dismissal – constructive dismissal is said to happen when an employer changes an employee's working conditions or job so unreasonably that the employee feels pressured into leaving the job. To prove constructive dismissal the employee must prove that the changes were unreasonable.

Unfair dismissal – this is a dismissal that the law considers unreasonable. While each case is judged on its merits dismissal for trade union membership, being of a particular race or religion or being homosexual are generally considered to be acts of unfair dismissal. If there is a dispute about whether or not a dismissal is fair employees can seek advice from, and be represented by, a trade union. The union might help them put their case to an industrial tribunal.

Redundancy

Redundancy occurs when the job an employee is doing is no longer required. This can be because the employer closes down a factory or office. It may be because the particular skills that an employee has are no longer required because the work of the firm has changed or the job can be done by fewer employees using new equipment or new processes.

Rather than make an employee **redundant** an employer might offer a similar job in the organisation. If it is a reasonable offer, made within four weeks of the employee's contract of employment being ended, the employee could lose their entitlement to redundancy pay if he or she turns it down.

redundant – employee is no longer required to work

Redundancy pay is paid by the employer with help from the government through the Redundancy Fund. Some employers add to the payment the redundant employee receives, depending upon their financial state and negotiations with the trade unions involved. Employers have a legal responsibility to provide the trade union with information about proposed redundancies and negotiate with them to minimise the effects of the redundancy.

Personal reasons

Employees may leave a job for reasons that have little to do with the employer. Examples include having to move to another part of the country, getting married or divorced, and illness.

Industrial relations

Another important part of Human Resources work is industrial relations – the discussion between representatives of the firm and representatives of the firm's employees. Usually the employees are represented in these discussions by a trade union official (see page 100). Industrial relations involves negotiation about many aspects of work:

- Wage and salary rates
- Health and Safety at work
- Training entitlement
- Working conditions
- Holiday entitlements
- Retirement arrangements
- Procedures for settling grievance or disciplinary matters
- Procedures for dealing with redundancy
- Hours of work.

Trade unions try to improve all these aspects of work for their members by negotiating with the business' representatives, who usually come from the Human Resources section. Unit Two has more details about human resources work.

Finance

All organisations need to look after their finances. Records of money coming into and leaving the business have to be kept. Just as importantly, businesses need to be able to understand their financial records to help them plan future activities and likely spending and income levels. In a small business the owner might look after the financial records. Usually firms pay someone to look after their accounts, perhaps on a part-time basis. Larger firms might have full-time staff looking after their finances. These people work in a separate department, usually referred to as the Finance Department or the Accounts Department. If the firm is large enough it will employ individuals to work within the department in particular roles.

Types of accountant

Financial accountants

These are usually found in large organisations. It is the responsibility of the Financial accountant to keep a record of what the company has spent and how this has affected its profits. He or she has to produce regular reports showing how the company's money has been spent and what income has been received. This information is vital as it helps the managers plan future activity. Regular financial reports can show patterns of expenditure or income that can be controlled or developed. The Financial accountant prepares the profit and loss account and balance sheet (see pages 167–68).

Cost accountants

The Cost accountant calculates the costs of the business's services and products. By showing which parts of the organisation are efficient he or she helps management make plans about how the work is to be organised. This is done by showing the costs of each part of the production process.

The Cost accountant is able to show which products are the most profitable, which helps managers decide on what to produce. The Cost accountant needs to work closely with the other departments to ensure that costs are measured as accurately as possible. Cost accountants help managers make decisions about the most efficient ways of running the firm.

Taking care of the firm's money is an important responsibility

Management accountants

The Management accountant deals with the actual income and expenditure of each of the firm's activities. Departments or sections of firms are often allocated money to perform their various tasks, and are set targets of how much they have to earn. These allocations and targets together are called a budget. The Management accountant advises managers about how well the various departments are meeting their budgets. This allows them to made decisions before, for example, a department spends too much.

When investigating your chosen business you could study how they:

- prepare accounts
- pay wages and salaries
- obtain capital and resources.

You need to get a good overview of how the finances of your companies are organised.

Administration and IT support

The term administration and IT support is used to cover a range of tasks, which include:

- clerical work (collecting and distributing mail, keeping records, organising meetings and responding to enquiries)
- cleaning and maintenance
- health and safety
- security
- support for software applications (word processing, payroll, accounts, databases, etc.), electronic communications and electronic transactions.

Clerical work

This deals with a variety of administrative tasks. School leavers taking a job for the first time often start with clerical work.

Mail

Look for examples of this sort of work in the business you study to show how it assists in the running of the business. You will find organisations generally receive mail in one of two ways:

- **Direct delivery** – the most common way is to deliver post direct to the firm's business address. In large firms the delivery will be to the firm's reception desk. The disadvantage of this approach is that work cannot start on the post until a delivery has been made.

- **Private box** – firms can rent a box at a local post office. Each box has a number that is part of the firm's address. Mail addressed to the firm's Post Office box (**PO box**) number is stored until collected by the firm's representative. This means that the firm can arrange to collect its mail at a time convenient to it, perhaps before most of the staff start work, so the post is ready to deal with at the start of the working day.

THE JARGON DRAGON

PO box – Post Office box, where a firm's mail is delivered and stored ready for collection

The procedures for opening mail vary according to the size of the firm. In small organisations the people to whom the letters are addressed will open them and deal with them directly. In larger firms the unopened letters will be sorted into piles for each department or people to whom they are addressed. Then the letters will be opened. In all but the smallest of organisations a secretary or a manager will open the letters and in the larger firms there will be a mail room to deal with incoming and outgoing mail.

Keeping records

Businesses store their records in a variety of ways – for example as photocopies or on computer disks. As the amount of information increases careful filing becomes important.

Filing

This is still the most common way of storing written papers. Written information is stored in filing cabinets or specially designed cupboards. The documents can be arranged in several ways:

- **Alphabetical** – this is rather like the way in which a telephone directory is organised. The name of the people who have written the documents, or the subject of the document, will be arranged according to where in the alphabet the first letter is (e.g. Barrett will be filed before Callaghan). If the first few letters are the same then the first different letter is used to decide where the document is filed (e.g. Monkey will be filed before Monks because the e in monkey comes before the s in monks in the alphabet).
- **Chronological** – in date or time order. Documents, usually letters, are placed according to the date they were sent or received. For example, letters sent in January will be filed before letters sent in June.

- **Geographical** – documents filed geographically are filed according to the county, town or country they were sent to or received from. The place names will be arranged alphabetically so that documents from Bristol will be found before documents from Coventry.

Logbooks

A logbook is used to record chosen activities, rather like a diary. The most common type of logbook used in business is probably the post book. This is used to record which letters have come into the firm and to whom they have been passed. A similar record of letters and parcels that have been sent out is also kept. Some offices have a system of recording who has taken files from one part of the building to another. Visitors to a business will be asked to sign in and out in a logbook. Logbooks are a helpful way of recording actions so that information can be tracked down when it is needed again.

References

The people who write certain types of business reports may get their information from other books, reports and people. By including references – in other words, by referring to where the information came from – the report allows the reader to check the actual references so that they can see if they come to the same opinions and conclusions as the writer of the report.

Organising meetings

Meetings vary in size from two people to a whole company of hundreds of people, although business meetings are usually small and more than 50 people is rare. Small meetings tend to be more efficient than larger ones. It is important to make sure that all the people who need to be involved are involved. A disadvantage of meetings is that they can be called too frequently and take staff away from other work. It is a bad habit to call meetings when other forms of communication can do the job just as well – for example, it is better to write an e-mail than to call staff together to hear a straightforward announcement. To be successful a meeting needs to be called well in advance to let people organise their time so they can attend.

The list of items to be discussed is written down in an **agenda**. The agenda is usually sent out before the meeting and contains details of the time, date, place of the meeting and items to be discussed. If an agenda is not sent then a **notice of meeting** should be sent.

THE JARGON DRAGON

agenda – list of items to be discussed at a meeting

notice of meeting – a memo containing details of time, place and date of a meeting

Meetings may vary in size from two people to a whole company

Most meetings have a 'chair' or 'chairperson' whose job it is to see that the meeting goes smoothly and that everyone gets a chance to contribute. Usually the chair will restrict the number of times a person can speak on any one topic. A secretary – male or female – takes a record of the meeting's decisions.

Cleaning and maintenance

Clean, well maintained premises are more pleasant and safer to work in and make a good impression on customers visiting the business. Administration is important in making sure that the working environment for employees is suitable and safe. Good administration will make sure the light, ventilation and heat in the work environment are suitable for the tasks being carried out. For example, people working with small items need bright light to avoid eyestrain. If you are working with chemicals that give off fumes good ventilation is essential. Escape routes and emergency exits must be kept clear at all times and clearly marked. On larger sites routes for traffic and pedestrians should be clearly marked and the two sorts of traffic kept separate.

Health and safety

Reporting accidents

Administration staff must ensure that there is a system in place for reporting accidents. Most businesses have an accident book or a special form to complete when an accident occurs.

Cleaning and maintenance can affect
what customers think of a business

The sort of information you will have to provide when reporting
an accident includes:

- who was injured
- what their injuries were
- who dealt with the matter
- names of witnesses
- date and time of accident
- what caused the accident
- how the accident was dealt with.

As many facts as possible should be reported. This helps planning
to avoid further incidents involving people or property. In
exceptional cases the report may be used if there is any legal
action as a result of the accident. You should always complete
any accident reports as soon as possible after the incident.

Avoiding accidents

- First-aid equipment should be available and kept in a clearly marked box or store.
- Where protective equipment is used it should be suitable for the job, approved to European Union standards and be clean and well maintained.
- There should be an adequate supply of drinking water and suitable toilets and sanitary arrangements.
- Office workers should avoid trailing wires across spaces between desks.
- Boxes and files should not be stacked on top of cupboards.
- Filing cabinet drawers should be shut after use – particularly the lower drawers, which people could easily walk into.
- When opening the top drawers of cabinets take care that the cabinet does not overbalance if it is heavily loaded.
- Computer screens should not be too dim or too bright, to avoid eyestrain.

Security

Making sure the firm's premises are safe and secure reduces loss through theft or damage. Damage to the premises means that levels of heating, lighting and ventilation may be reduced to unsafe or uncomfortable levels. Simple precautions such as locking filing cabinets, cupboards, doors and windows at the end of the day help security. Employees should follow the security systems that are in place – for example, by making sure that burglar alarms are turned on when necessary.

Support for software applications

The widespread use of computers in business means that a system is needed to help employees deal with them. Some firms will employ specialist technical staff whose job it is to ensure that computers and software operate as intended. Large firms will sometimes employ an outside organisation to take care of its computer support needs.

THE JARGON DRAGON

software applications – computer programs used for certain tasks, e.g. word processors or spreadsheets

case study

Dunlop

For over 40 years, Dunlop has been one of the world's leading manufacturers of equipment for tennis, squash and badminton. At the end of 2000, five of the world's top 25 tennis players were using Dunlop's racquets. The company has always used technology to maintain its leading position.

In the mid 1980s, Dunlop began to use factories in Taiwan. The reduced cost in manufacturing allowed new designs and features to be introduced. In 1990, a large investment was made in a 3-D CAD system to allow the Marketing Department to see what racquets would look before the design was sent to the Far East. At this time, it was usual for a model to be made in the UK using traditional techniques, but these models gave no reliable indication of weight or performance.

By the mid 1990s, production of tennis racquets had moved to Taiwan. Dunlop used the knowledge and low costs of Taiwan to speed up development and take the time from design to completion of racquet frames down to around three months.

In 1999, Paul Angell joined Dunlop as a Development Engineer. He introduced a new CAD system, PowerSHAPE from Delcam. PowerSHAPE is used to design and model the racquets in the UK, before sending the finished design to Taiwan by e-mail. The time from completing the design to the delivery of the first racquet was reduced from three months to nine weeks!

The first model to benefit from this new approach was the Inferno, a novel design with a unique 'hot-melt' graphite skin layered over the whole frame. This new manufacturing technique gives players more power and better control from an extremely light racquet.

Based on an article at: `http://www.delcam.com`

Q1 *What had Dunlop always done to maintain its leading position?*

Q2 *By the mid-1990s, what had been the effect of moving production to Taiwan and introducing computer-aided design (CAD)?*

Q3 *What was the effect of introducing the CAD system PowerSHAPE?*

Q3 *Why would e-mail be used to send the designs to Taiwan?*

Operations

In some organisations the work of the operations section will overlap with those of the administration section. Operations is about the firm making the best use of the resources it has available:

- Buildings and land – offices, shops or farmland
- Equipment – vehicles, computers and machinery
- People – operators, managers, support staff and specialists
- Materials – products for retailing or raw materials.

Many businesses will use computers to improve their operations. This may involve computer-aided design (CAD), which helps speed up the design process, and the use of robots in manufacturing goods (computer-aided manufacturing, also known as CAM).

FIND IT OUT

Visit your local job centre or school/college careers library. Identify ten jobs and say which of them fit into the types described in this chapter.

Quality control is an important feature of business activity. Firms should have systems in place to check thoroughly that their activities and finished products meet the standards they set themselves.

Quality systems can give customers confidence in a firm's products or services

Boots the Chemist, for example, ensure quality by carrying out more than half a million tests each year on about 6000 products, over 4000 raw materials and 15 000 different packaging items. By reducing the amount of unsatisfactory output the company ensures that customers are more likely to use their products or services again.

Businesses can prove that they meet quality standards in producing goods and services by obtaining quality standard ISO 9002. A firm that wants to show it has good quality systems for managing and training staff might ask to be assessed for the Investors in People (IIP) award (see page 121). For both these awards external assessors will visit the firm and check their systems and records. If they meet the required standards the company will be awarded a certificate and allowed to use the quality symbol on its advertisements and other documents. The business will be checked again in future to ensure standards are still being met.

Marketing and sales

This section of a company helps the managers to understand what their customers want. It does this by:

- Market research
- Promotion
- Sales.

Market research

Before a company produces a new product it needs to know what its customers want and what its rivals are offering. The way in which a firm finds out about the behaviour of its customers and its rivals is called market research. It will use this information to make sure that its promotion and sales activities are designed to reach the people it is aiming to reach. When you examine the businesses involved in your research find out how these activities are carried out and how they link to the business' aims. Pay particular attention to how IT is used.

Only the largest of businesses will employ their own market researchers. This very specialised activity is usually done by market research agencies such as MORI or Gallup or advertising agencies such as J Walter Thompson.

By researching the market as much as possible firms try to reduce the risk of an unprofitable investment in a new product. Market research is also used to find out what customers think about existing products and services by asking questions like:

- What does the customer prefer?
- How many people will buy our new product?
- How can we reach the consumer?
- What are customers prepared to pay?
- What packaging is best?
- How might customer tastes change?
- What do our rivals produce?
- What are their prices?
- What are our rivals likely to do in future?

Market research examines the probable behaviour of other firms and potential customers.

The information obtained in market research is either primary data or secondary data.

Primary data

Primary data is new information that is directly related to the new product the firm hopes to introduce. Primary data is obtained through interviews, questionnaires, observation or experiment. Some firms use consumer panels, which are groups of consumers who agree to taste or test new products and complete questionnaires giving their opinion.

THE JARGON DRAGON

market research – the way in which a firm finds out about the behaviour of its customers and rivals

primary data – data from market research directly related to a new product

secondary data – information already collected, which is used for further market analysis

Useful market research can be
conducted outside the company

THE JARGON DRAGON

test market – selling and
advertising a new product
in a small area to test market
reaction

Before getting involved in the expense of national advertising and
distribution of a new product firms will often **test market** the
product. This is done by selling and advertising the product in
only one region of the country, usually linking it to advertising on
the local commercial television network. Sales figures will be
analysed and a judgement made about the suitability of the
product for national launch.

The research that obtains primary data is called field research
because it happens away from the firm ('in the field'). Primary
data is usually the most useful data as the research is aimed at
answering particular questions to which the firm needs answers.
The disadvantage is that it is the most expensive sort of research
to undertake and is often slow to produce results.

Secondary data

Secondary data is information that has already been collected,
which is interpreted to find answers to the firm's questions.
Sources of secondary data include reference books, magazines,
websites, and government statistics such as *Social Trends*.
Information the firm already has – such as past sales figures, the
number of faulty goods returned or letters from satisfied
customers – is also secondary data. Secondary data is gathered
through desk research, so called because it can be carried out by
analysing existing information at a desk inside the organisation.

Promotion

Promotion and advertising are often confused. *Advertising* involves persuading or informing the public about something while *promotion* is about giving the consumer 'something for nothing' in the hope that it will encourage future sales. An important part of selling is to persuade customers to try a product for the first time. The main aim of sales promotion is to break down this reluctance.

Sales promotion techniques

These include:

- **Free samples** – small packages of the product may be given away free. The idea is that once the customer has tried the new product they will want to use it again and so buy it. The product may be given away in shops, on the street or delivered to houses. Sometimes cosmetics are distributed free with women's magazines.

- **Free gifts** – free gifts, such as tee shirts or sports bags, can be obtained by sending proof of purchase to the manufacturer. This type of promotion operates on the same principle as competitions as it aims to increase sales

Many companies use sales promotion techniques to increase sales

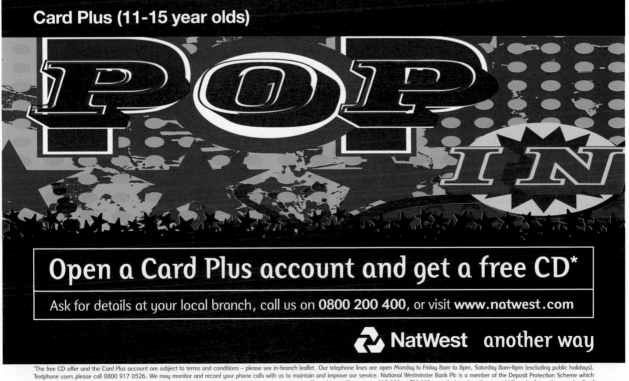

through attractive gifts. The free gift will often have the manufacturer's name on it. This provides free advertising in future. A mail-order catalogue, for example, might offer a free gift, such as a camera or set of pans, to encourage people to use the catalogue. The aim here is to persuade the customer to join something where future purchases will be easy and so more likely.

- **Coupons** – coupons are often printed in press advertisements or leaflets. They allow the customer a price reduction on the next purchase of a particular item. Customers reluctant to buy at the full price may be willing to buy at a reduced price. The idea is that once the customer has tried the new product they will wish to use it again and so buy it at full price next time.

- **Competitions** – the chance to win a holiday, car, house, stereo or some other luxury item can attract a lot of attention. Often a condition of entry is to prove that you have used the manufacturer's product by sending a number of labels or ring pulls with the entry. The manufacturer aims to make the prize attractive enough so that people will buy the product in order to enter the competition.

Sales

The number of sales any business makes will depend on how easy it is for the customer to buy. This means having opening hours that suit the customer, using clear displays and demonstrations and keeping queues short. Offering credit and

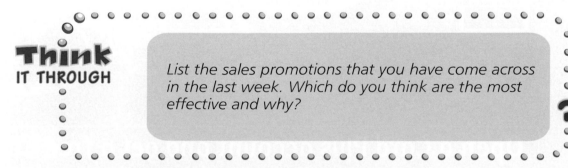

Think IT THROUGH

List the sales promotions that you have come across in the last week. Which do you think are the most effective and why?

allowing payment by cheque, debit or credit card also help the customer to make a purchase. Helpful sales staff are important if the firm is to make sales – not just staff in shops but travelling sales staff who sell goods to shops or staff who take orders over the telephone.

Computers are widely used to promote sales in business. The Internet, for example, has increased sales opportunities – and stores such as Tesco encourage customers to place orders for their groceries over the Internet and then deliver the goods to the customer's home (see www.tesco.com/shopping/). Some retailers, such as Amazon, do not have traditional stores but sell entirely over the Internet (see www.amazon.co.uk).

Internet retailing with companies such as Tesco makes purchasing easier for the customer

What are the advantages and disadvantages of the move to Internet retailing from the point of view of (a) the retailer; (b) the customer; (c) traditional shop workers?

Think
IT THROUGH

THE JARGON DRAGON

EFTPOS – electronic method of collecting payment

Supermarkets and petrol stations use loyalty card schemes that award points to customers according to how much they spend. As well as being a type of promotion they help the seller to track what customers are buying (and when) and ensure that stock levels meet customer needs.

Both credit cards and debit cards make use of Electronic Funds Transfer at Point of Sale (<u>EFTPOS</u>) through computers. When making a purchase the customer presents their debit or credit card to the sales assistant, who passes it through an electronic reader to transfer funds from the shopper's account to the retailer's account (see page 149).

The availability of cash points or cash machines outside banks and in supermarkets, petrol stations and motorway service areas means that customers can use electronic transfer of funds to pay in or transfer money to different accounts.

Customer service

Service to customers can be the deciding factor when a customer is choosing between rival firms (see page 121). Successful businesses provide a range of services for their customers.

Information

Customers will ask for information before they make a purchase so that they can compare rival products. The price of the item is an important piece of information. Questions about the performance of the item are also sometimes asked, e.g. 'How many miles per gallon will this car do?' 'Are these boots waterproof?' Customers also seek information about environmental or 'green' concerns – e.g. 'Does the product have side effects that damage the environment?' 'Was the item tested on animals?'

Advice

When buying something for the first time customers will ask for guidance from sales staff, who they expect to know something about the items for sale and the alternatives available. This need for advice is most common with expensive or complicated items such as cars, video players and computers. A sales assistant who makes helpful comments and simplifies the situation will help the customer make a decision to buy. When offering advice the sales assistant should be able to show the customer how far the items on sale meet his or her needs. A person who feels they have received honest helpful information is more likely to be a satisfied customer and make recommendations to friends or buy from you again.

Delivery

A delivery service is another example of what a firm can do to make it easier for a customer to make a purchase. This is particularly important with large or bulky items such as cookers, televisions, refrigerators or beds. However, grocers, butchers and newsagents often offer a delivery service for small items to make shopping more convenient for their customers. Sometimes a delivery service is free or at a low cost to encourage customers to make a purchase. The most expensive part of a delivery service is the wages of the delivery staff. For this reason some shops, for example B+Q and Ikea, lend or hire roof racks or vehicles to customers for them to use to take their purchases home.

Businesses buying large quantities from other businesses find transport costs are expensive and will also be attracted to suppliers who are able to offer a free or low-cost delivery service.

After-sales service

How well a customer is treated after they have bought an item is almost as important as how well they are treated before they make the purchase. Expensive or complicated items are more likely to be offered with an after-sales service.

Research and development

THE JARGON DRAGON

product life cycle – pattern of sales after launching a new product

Unless a firm is continually improving and developing its product range it cannot succeed. Once a firm has launched a new product or service, if things go to plan sales will gradually increase. But there will come a point where sales level off and then decline. This sequence is known as the **product life cycle**. Declining sales mean reduced income for the business. Businesses are always looking to develop new products or relaunch old ones with some changes that are attractive to customers. Because of this many large firms have Research and Development (R & D) departments. These, usually small, sections aim to come up with new ideas to improve either the design of the product or the performance of the product. In attempting to suggest improvements and changes the R & D section must bear in mind three considerations.

The three 'p's

- **Price** – any new ideas they have must be capable of being produced at a price consumers are prepared to pay.
- **Practicality** – new ideas developed in a laboratory or at a designer's desk are one thing. Making them in large quantities is something else. The new idea is only useful if it can be done on a commercial scale. Another consideration is that the idea is only practical if the consumer is likely to buy the product.
- **Profit** – any new idea will only be developed by the firm if it is profitable. There is often a conflict between the consumer's need and the firm's need to make a profit.

These three pressures show how the R & D section needs to be in touch with the Marketing Department as well as the Manufacturing section of the business. Links with Personnel are obvious when it comes to recruiting highly qualified staff to work in this area. Monitoring costs of development make links with the Finance section important. The need for communication with Marketing is great as no new product can be successful unless there is a demand for it.

Boots No. 7 Brand of cosmetics was first launched in 1935. In the early 1990s the No. 7 brand was a mid-market product, but sales had stopped growing. Both the teenage budget (low cost) and premium (high price) markets were expanding. The product was seen to be good quality but drab and old-fashioned.

Boots decided to relaunch the No. 7 brand as a **premium product**, premium products being those that sell at a high price. Research and development had allowed a substantial range of claims to be made for the products such as 'not tested on animals' and 'hypoallergenic'. Two-thirds of the colour range was new and every possible new idea was incorporated. There was lots of customer testing against competitors in the new market to ensure that products in the range out-performed their rivals. Finally, the packaging was redesigned to give greater visual appeal, compare favourably in both appearance and usability with other premium products, and have a long-lasting image.

Based on an article at http://www.bized.ac.uk/ compfact/boots/ boots23.htm

Q1 *When was Boots No. 7 Brand first launched?*

Q2 *How did the firm check whether the new product could do well against its rivals?*

Q3 *What is the advantage to the firm of selling cosmetics in the 'premium' market?*

THE JARGON DRAGON

online – working through the Internet

Online support for customers

A lot of companies use their websites to help their customers online. Software companies, such as Microsoft, will help customers by putting information on their websites about software developments, correction of faults, information and queries about how to use their programs. A number of companies correct errors in their programs by sending amendments, or patches, to customers via their website. Online facilities provided by parcel firms such as Fed-Ex allow customers to track where in the world their parcel or package is. Airport websites provide details of arrival and departure times of flights. You can also check train times online.

Electronic transactions

Computers can help sales by processing payments. Unit 3 describes how computers can be used for stock control. The barcode system allows computers to 'read' the information about products and register this with the till in the supermarket and the stock records in the warehouse. Previously these tasks were done on paper by clerical staff.

Barcodes and computers make stock management much faster

Business communications

Employees in a business must communicate:

- within their functional area
- outside their functional area, and
- outside of the business.

Communication can take place in a number of ways. The major ones are listed below:

- Oral communication
- Video communication
- Written communication
- Graphical communication.

Each of these methods has advantages and disadvantages according to the sort of information being communicated.

Oral communication

Spoken, oral or verbal communication can take many forms – in an interview, at a meeting or in a telephone call, for instance. Telephone calls are usually made from one person to another but in order to save the time and money involved in organising meetings a number of businesses now use telephone conferences. Several people from different parts of the world are connected by telephone at the same time and can speak to each other.

Oral communication in an office environment can take many forms

jargon – specialist terms or phrases used in a particular industry (e.g. computing or nursing)

In any oral communication it is important to speak clearly. Avoid using slang and <u>jargon</u> unless it actually helps others to understand. Bear in mind the background of the person listening to you to judge how much they will understand.

Spoken communication has the advantage of being fast and immediate. The response or feedback is almost instant when the person you are speaking to hears what you are saying. This form of communication allows questions to be raised and answered quickly. Verbal communication speeds up the consideration of different opinions through discussion. The disadvantages of verbal communication methods are that they do not allow the same detailed level of preparation and presentation as written methods and an accurate record is hard to obtain.

The telephone is important to spoken communication as it allows rapid communication over long distances. It has the disadvantage of being more expensive than most written methods of communication.

Verbal communication is a good way of getting a quick response to your comments

Video communication

Video conferencing allows people in different parts of the world to see and talk to each other without the expense of travelling to a meeting. Specialist video conferencing equipment can be purchased or hired from specialist firms. Modern computers can be fitted with webcams, cameras that can broadcast pictures over the Internet. The quality of webcams is not normally as good as video conferencing equipment but does allow long-distance communication.

One disadvantage of video communication equipment is that it is expensive. However, if the equipment is used regularly as an alternative to sending people to meetings the savings and convenience are generally considered an advantage. Video communication provides the convenience and speed of oral communication and the face-to-face contact of meetings without people having to travel.

Written communication

This can take many forms. Letters, memos, advertisements, reports and e-mail are examples of written communication.

Letters

Letters are used by a company to communicate with people and organisations outside the firm. They are *not* used for communication within the firm. The highest standards of presentation and spelling are important if a letter is to make a good impression. For this reason it should be typed or word-processed on high-quality paper. Most firms have their name, address and business symbol (their logo) printed at the top or bottom of their <u>headed paper</u>. It is common to include the name of the company chairman or main directors.

THE JARGON DRAGON

headed paper – paper with the company name, address and logo printed on

An example of a well-presented letter is shown on page 48. As the example letter shows, the address of the person receiving the letter should always be typed on the letter. The title of the person should be used as well as their name – for example, Mr G. Smith, Dr P.J. Rowbotham, Lord Lucan, Ms M. Callaghan (Chief Personnel Officer). The address on the letter should match exactly the address on the envelope. The town should be printed in capitals and the post code given. Many letters have a reference number or code on them. This is used to identify who wrote and typed the letter but may include any reference numbers the firm uses, such as the person's credit account number. The person receiving the letter is known as the addressee. If possible, the letter should be started using the addressee's name (e.g. Dear Ms Goggins, Dear Mr Malik, Dear Peter, Dear Sue). The letter should be broken down into paragraphs to deal with each of the points or lines of argument being made. Paragraphs break down the information into manageable parts and so aid understanding.

If the letter starts with 'Dear Sir' or 'Dear Madam' you should end it with 'Yours faithfully', but if you started with the person's name ('Dear Jamie', 'Dear Dr Jones') then you should end with 'Yours sincerely'. Leave space at the end for the sender's signature and then type their name, followed by their job title (for instance, John Whitley, Credit Controller or Reema Salim, Finance Director).

If something else has been included in the envelope with the letter, such as an application form, leaflet or price list, 'Enc' is typed about two centimetres below the signature. 'Enc' is short for 'enclosure' and tells the addressee that something has been sent with the letter.

Well-designed headed paper will create a good impression of the business

nelson thornes

Delta Place
27 Bath Road
Cheltenham GL53 7TH
United Kingdom

t +44 (0) 1242 267100
f +44 (0) 1242 221914
e mail@nelsonthornes.com
w www.nelsonthornes.com

Mr J. Cartwright
10 Church Street
CHELTENHAM
Gloucestershire
GL53 6PY

19 February 2002

Dear Mr Cartwright

Applied Business GCSE (Double Award)

Thank you for writing to us and sending some samples of your illustration work. They are definitely the kind of style that we are looking for.

Memos

A memo is the most common form of written communication used to pass on messages from one part of the business to another. Memos are not sent to people outside the organisation – letters are used to do that. Memos are written on specially designed memo forms. Memos are usually polite, brief, direct and to the point. Longer memos may have paragraphs, or each point made numbered. Notice that memos are not usually signed, and do not begin with 'Dear ....'.

Letters and memos both provide a record of what has been communicated and allow the person writing them to prepare the presentation and wording before sending the message. The disadvantage of these methods of communication is that both the sending and the time taken to receive a reply make them unsuitable for situations requiring swift action.

Reports

When detailed consideration of a subject is needed it is usual for a report to be produced. An individual, or group, will be asked to produce a report for a particular date. This date is the deadline. It is important that deadlines are met as failure to do so may delay the work of others. Each business will have its own style for reports but the following features are common.

- Each paragraph should be numbered.
- **A title explaining the purpose of the report** – e.g. 'A report on the reasons for reduced sales at the Nuneaton branch during the last year' or 'A report to investigate the most suitable word processor for the new Wallsend office'.
- **A summary** – if the person receiving the report is likely to be too busy to read it all or if the report is very long, a summary should be used. The summary is a short section at the front of the report which gives brief details of the investigation, the recommendations and the reasons behind them. It sums up the report and is written last.
- **Terms of reference** – this is a paragraph explaining what the people preparing the report were asked to do and who the report is to be presented to. Here is an example: 'Joe Brayson, Carol Smith and Ian Glover were asked to investigate word processors costing less than £1000 to find which would be the most suitable for the new Wallsend office. The report was to be presented to Peter Anderson by Friday 23 July.'
- **Methods followed to complete the task** – who was interviewed? What books were consulted? What was done in the course of the research? Which firms were asked to supply price lists? This section will normally take more than one paragraph.
- **Results of the investigation** – this should be a straightforward factual account of the results. Who said what, costs of each of the alternatives being considered, facilities of each machine, cost of servicing, ease of operation, whether they can be linked to other machines, etc.

- **A conclusion** – this states what the results lead you to believe. For example, that WING word processors are cheap but STRADAMs are more reliable while AMIGO do not produce a word processor to suit the needs of your business. MBI processors can be used with other computers but are difficult to learn.
- **Recommendations** – for example, after considering the various word-processing machines available the writers recommend one particular machine.
- **An appendix** – if there are a lot of complicated details these may be presented in an appendix at the end of the report. It is important to refer to the appendix at suitable points in the results and conclusion sections of the report.

E-mail

This is a quick way of communicating. E-mails are usually polite, brief, direct and to the point, but can also be quite informal. Documents such as letters, spreadsheets or databases can be attached to the e-mail for the reader to look at if more lengthy communication is needed. Pictures and sound files can also be sent this way. An e-mail is a good way of sending urgently needed written or visual communications and is cheap to use. The disadvantage is that both sender and receiver need access to computer equipment and a telephone line in order to communicate. This can be expensive to set up.

E-mail is a fast and convenient method of communication

| File Edit Mailbox Message Transfer Special Window Scripts Help |

Paul Starling, 1:39 pm +0000, Project Meeting

Send

To: Paul Starling <p.starling@metalwidgets.co.uk>
From: Joanne Derwent <j.derwent@metalwidgets.co.uk> head office
Subject: Project Meeting
Cc:
Bcc:
X-Attachments: agenda.doc locationreport.doc

Paul

Please find attached the agenda for Thursday's meeting.

Item two is a discussion on the report we commissioned on the proposed locations for the new manufacturing site, this is also attached.

I look forward to hearing your comments on the report.

Joanne

Graphical communication

This means the use of pictures or diagrams. It can include plans of a building, signs, charts showing sales in previous years, notices on a notice board or web pages. Good graphical communication can communicate ideas more simply than written words and can be understood by people who do not have a good grasp of English.

External influences

As well as having to operate efficiently inside the business, managers, staff and owners have to deal with influences from outside the business, such as:

- business competitors
- economic conditions or
- environmental constraints.

Business competitors

Business activity involves competition to persuade customers to buy one firm's products rather than another's. Once a sale has been made the wise business will try to make repeat sales and keep its customers. In order to be competitive businesses should pay particular attention to price, quality and availability. Customers generally wish to pay the lowest possible price for a product but may be prepared to pay more for one if it is of better quality than similar items. They may be willing to pay more if the higher priced goods are easier to obtain. For example, small local shops tend to be more expensive than large out-of-town supermarkets but the small shops survive because they are more convenient, being local.

Imagine you are looking for your perfect partner in the personal ads. If your dream date is between the ages of 25 and 34 earning more than £50 000, look no further than the *Financial Times*. This paper has the youngest readership of any of the broadsheet newspapers. Its wealthy readers work hard and play hard. If you prefer going to the pub, listening to music and watching football, you are more likely to find your ideal mate reading the *Sun* or the *Star*.

These stereotypes highlight the fact that 'we are what we read', and vice versa. Our research shows that if you enjoy a heated political debate, you should invite *FT* and *Guardian* readers to your dinner parties. These types are three times more likely than the national average to have an interest in current affairs. If, however, you are on the lookout for a DIY enthusiast, your perfect partner is likely to read the *Sun*. According our research, *Sun* readers come out on top when it comes to being practical around the home.

The once essential service of having a paper delivered to your home daily is now mainly used by the older generations. Retired people, in particular, have more time available to read a paper regularly and may be less able to go to the shops to collect it. For younger people, buying a paper on the way to work is as much a part of the daily routine as picking up the paper from the doormat is to their grandparents. The trend reflects the time-pressured nature of today's society, causing workers to leave home earlier and travel longer.

Finally, however much a person's cultural, social or economic background influences his or her choice newspaper, one thing unites everyone – a love of food. Our research found all readers, whatever their favourite paper, enjoyed cooking and eating out. So, if your ideal partner is a budding chef, you have a good chance of finding them in the personal ads page of any newspaper.

Based on an article at: http://media.guardian.co.uk/marketingandpr/pulse/story/0,10489,595988,00.html

Q1 *What are the features of* Financial Times *readers according to this research?*

Q2 *What activities do* Sun *readers prefer?*

Q3 *What is the difference between the way young readers buy a paper and how older readers get their copy?*

Q4 *Given the different sorts of readers, how might the price and type of goods advertised in these papers be different?*

Consider an item of clothing such as a sweatshirt. Which brands would you buy if you had the money? Which brands would you definitely not buy? What are the reasons for your decision? Are price, quality or availability important?

?

Think
IT THROUGH

Business customers

When a business is considering its customers it should know about several important things.

FIND IT OUT

Look in a travel agents, bank or newspaper and note daily for a week how much you will have to pay to receive: 1000 Japanese Yen (¥), 5 USA Dollars ($), 10 Euros (€).

THE JARGON DRAGON

exchange rate – how much of one currency can be exchanged for another

Exchange rates

If firms in the UK sell goods and services overseas they will expect to be paid in pounds (£). If they buy goods from overseas they will have to pay in the currency of the country from which they are making the purchase. How much of one currency people are prepared to exchange for another is called the <u>exchange rate</u>. This means that the pound has a value in relation to other currencies such as the dollar ($). The value of the pound in relation to overseas currencies affects the ability of British producers to sell overseas and import goods into Britain. If the value of the pound is too high foreign purchasers will not be able to afford British goods or services. On the other hand, British firms will be able to cheaply import goods. A low pound has the opposite effect.

Currency exchange rates can sometimes change quickly

The government can influence the exchange rate by selling or buying foreign currency or pounds. Making more pounds available (selling) drives the price down (lowers the exchange rate) while buying raises the price. In this case price is merely the exchange rate. The government has to find an exchange rate level that is helpful to both importers and exporters – the firms who sell goods and services overseas. One of the reasons several European countries have started to use the Euro as currency (€) is to reduce the uncertainties caused by changes in exchange rates.

Government in the UK is expected to do what it can to help the economy grow so that business and the general public can plan their future saving and spending.

? *Joan Anderson runs a cycle repair business and imports the parts she needs from China, France and India. She needs to buy a new workbench and tools in the next two months and plans to borrow the money from her bank. How would a rise in interest rates and a fall in the exchange rates affect her?*

Think
IT THROUGH

Environmental constraints

Business activity can damage the environment. The government and the European Union have introduced laws to reduce the impact of business activity on the environment. In the UK these laws are overseen by local councils, working with a government body called the Environment Agency (`www.environment-agency.gov.uk/`). The government department that oversees all of this activity is the Department for Environment, Food and Rural Affairs (`http://www.defra.gov.uk`). A number of companies have developed an environmental policy that shows what they are doing to reduce the effect of their activities on the environment.

Unless it is carefully controlled, business activity can cause:

- air pollution
- noise pollution
- water pollution
- wasteful use of resources.

Air pollution

Growth in business activity led to a rise in air pollution during the 20th century. In London in 1952 around 4000 people died due to poor quality air, known as smog. Laws to improve the air quality followed soon afterwards. Carbon dioxide and methane from businesses play a major role in increasing global warming (the greenhouse effect) and damaging the atmosphere. The government wants to reduce air pollution levels to a more healthy level. They intend to do this through laws such as the Environmental Protection Act, which strengthens controls over industrial air quality. The law is enforced by local authorities and the Environment Agency.

Businesses are also guided to control air pollution through the Climate Change Levy. This is a tax on energy use by UK businesses. It is intended to encourage the efficient use of energy and create job opportunities. The UK has set itself a target to ensure that carbon dioxide emissions in 2010 are 20% lower than the 1990 levels.

Noise pollution

Noise pollution is covered by the Environmental Protection Act. The Act tries to control disturbance caused by noise and vibration, which is created in any premises. Businesses near residential properties need to take particular care that they do not disturb their neighbours. The local council will investigate complaints of noise pollution. This could be loud music from a club or machinery noise from a factory. At first, the environmental health officer (EHO) will decide whether the noise is a nuisance and try to resolve the matter informally. If this informal approach fails, then the EHO can serve an abatement notice on the business making the noise. The notice states that the noise nuisance must stop and gives details of what must be done to stop it. If the business does not comply with the notice it commits a criminal offence, and the owner or manager responsible may be taken to court. A business that disobeys the law can be fined up to £20 000. The EHO may remove the noise-making equipment if the noise does not stop.

As a company we take great pride in our commitment to environmental policies which are designed to minimise the impact of the network in both rural and urban areas. Vodafone has an environmental policy statement that covers its operations and their impact on the environment. The main elements are:

- *to use technology that is not known to be harmful to people or the environment.*
- *to endeavour only to purchase environmentally friendly products*
- *to endeavour to recycle waste wherever practical*
- *to minimise the use of harmful CFCs*
- *to preserve areas of nature conservation*
- *to ensure all reasonable efforts are made to minimise the visual impact of the Company's equipment.*

Based on an item at http://www.vodafone.co.uk

Q1 *What is the advantage of recycling waste?*

Q2 *Using your knowledge of mobile telephones, consider in what ways Vodafone's activities might damage the environment if not properly controlled?*

Q3 *Why might a company publicise its environmental policy?*

Water pollution

Water is an essential part of most forms of energy production, agriculture and many industrial processes and is important in sanitation, cleaning, catering and heating. Only around 3% of drinking water is actually used for drinking and cooking. Many business activities create waste and pollute water that has to be cleaned or disposed of. Firms that pollute water supplies can be prosecuted by the Environment Agency and fined by the courts.

Water supply and disposal costs add to business costs. According to the Environment Agency a typical office may have an annual water bill of over £2000. Water-saving schemes will save money by reducing the costs of supply and disposal and lead to savings because energy use is reduced. The University of Liverpool, for example, fitted automatic controls to toilet flushers in toilets at its halls of residence. This cost a one-off investment of £60 000 but saved over £95 000 per year and reduced water consumption by over 50%.

Businesses must deal with many external pressures

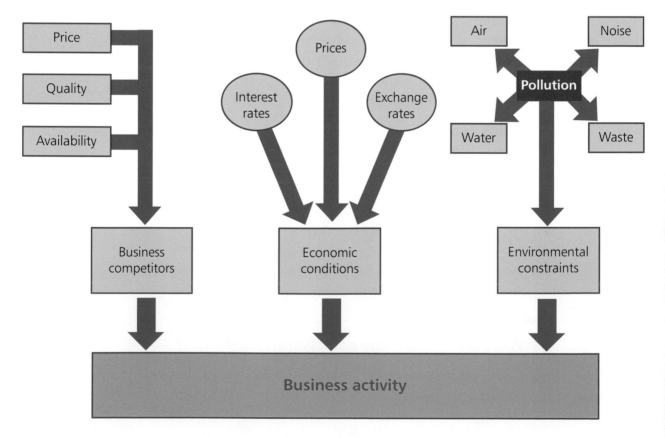

Wasteful use of resources

Wasteful use of resources should be avoided for both financial and environmental reasons. Resources that leave the firm as waste cannot be sold or earn money for the business. Only finished products earn money. Reducing waste leads to more cost-effective production. For example, Walkers Snack Foods put in place a waste reduction strategy. This made them more efficient and saved them over £960 000. Pilkington's Tiles found 29 ways to reduce waste and made savings of nearly £500 000. Reducing waste also reduces the impact the business has on the environment.

Recycling is one way of dealing with waste. The best way is not to create it in the first place

What's in this unit?

People are essential in helping a business to achieve its aims – they are the most important part of the business. This unit talks about the roles individuals have in a business – the things they have to do – and how employers and employees can work together. You will learn how businesses recruit staff and train their employees. This will help you when you finish your studies and start work. You will, for instance, learn about your rights and responsibilities, as well learning about what employers have to consider when dealing with their staff. In other words you will find out about what you are entitled to, as well as what is expected of you.

Good working relationships, communication, organisation and clear responsibilities are essential to business success. This unit helps you consider how these things can be achieved and what you can contribute. The Human Resources Department, sometimes called the Personnel Department, is an important part of any medium-sized or large firm. Here, you will find out about how this department works. Computers and other forms of technology are changing how work is organised and how people communicate. You will need to understand the impact of this technology as part of your studies.

This unit will show you how businesses organise themselves to communicate with their customers. You will also find out about how businesses use Customer Service Departments to ensure that customers are treated fairly and within the law and how information technology has helped businesses to reach their customers directly.

People and Business 2

In this unit you will learn about:

Stakeholders

A business's **stakeholders** are the people who are affected by the actions of the business. Some of the main stakeholders are discussed in this section.

Customers

Customers are the people who buy the firm's goods or services. When you pay for a bus ride you are a customer of the bus company, and the bus company you use is a customer of the firm that sells buses to them. Customers want a business to produce the goods or services they want at a price they can afford, when and where they want them. They expect to be treated politely, promptly and fairly. Sometimes they expect advice about items before they buy them and support after they have bought them.

Customers can influence a business by how much they choose to spend. Some customers refuse to buy from a particular company because they are unhappy about some aspect of its business dealings. This is called a customer boycott and can harm a business because it reduces its income.

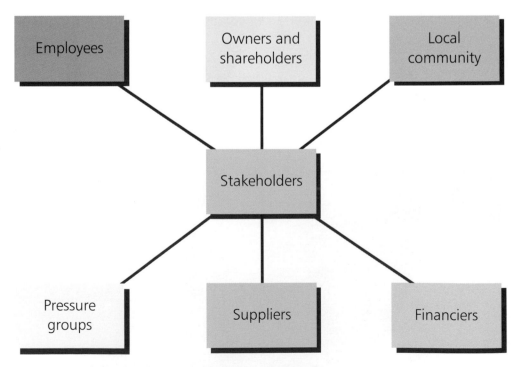

These are some of the stakeholders affected by business activities

Customers can influence a business by how much they choose to spend

Employees

Anyone with a **contract of employment** who works for a business, including its managers, is an employee of the company. Sensible employees know they will be affected by the success of the business they work for – a successful business will maintain their employment and give them an income from wages.

Employees expect to have reasonably comfortable and safe working conditions. They expect to be consulted about changes that will affect them and to be treated fairly. Employees can influence a business by being reliable and doing what is expected of them. Contributing ideas and suggestions is another way of influencing the firm's success.

THE JARGON DRAGON

contract of employment – legal agreement describing terms of employment

Employees are important stakeholders in any business

According to employers, employees of a successful business need many skills, such as:

- number
- communication
- IT
- solving problems
- working with others
- improving their own learning and skills.

If employees feel unfairly treated they can influence the business by refusing to work (going on **strike**).

This means the business' production will be disrupted and income from sales will be lost.

THE JARGON DRAGON

strike – refusal of employees to work, as part of a dispute with an employer

Owners and shareholders

These are the people who own the business (see page 6). They are interested in the business making a profit and giving them income in return for investing money in the business. Owners and shareholders expect their employees to be reasonable in their dealings and their suppliers and customers to be honest. Owners and shareholders can influence the business and other stakeholders by the amount they invest and where they choose to locate their business.

Owners and shareholders can influence the business by the decisions they make

The **CBI** today said it was 'deeply concerned' by European Parliament proposals to strengthen new laws on worker consultation.

The CBI is particularly worried by proposals to:

- allow employee representatives to delay business decisions even where extensive consultation has already taken place
- force companies to consult worker representatives before managers have come to a view on ideas affecting the workforce.

John Cridland, Deputy Director General, said: 'Successful businesses have to make decisions work quickly and these changes would simply throw a spanner in the works. We strongly believe in proper consultation but these proposals are a recipe for grinding business decision making to a halt

'We are very encouraged that the European Union has said it would be "unwise" to depart from the current finely balanced common position. We will work closely with the UK government to prevent them being adopted by the **Council of Ministers**.'

Based on an article on the Confederation of British Industry (CBI) website http://www.cbi.org.uk/ **October, 2001**

Q1 *What disadvantages might there be from making employers consult workers about business decisions?*

Q2 *What advantages could there be from making employers consult their workers?*

Q3 *Is it right that business decisions should be delayed if workers disagree with employers?*

The local community

People in the local community will be interested in the business as a place where they can get jobs and the sort of environmental effects it will have. Other local businesses will be interested in opportunities to become suppliers (see page 69). The local community will expect the business to be considerate in regard to noise or atmospheric pollution and the impact of its activities on the area. It can influence the business by letting the owners know how its activities are affecting them and by creating publicity about the firm's activities. This publicity may have a positive or negative effect on sales.

The government

Government is interested in businesses because they provide jobs for the population and provide government income from taxes. Local government (your local council) tries to represent the views of the local community. National government (parliament) looks after matters of national concern.

Businesses are sometimes involved in research into products and services that can make people happier or healthier and contribute to economic well-being. Government will expect businesses to pay their taxes and obey the laws about customer protection, the environment and treatment of their employees. The laws decided by government will affect business activity – for example, laws about consumer protection will influence how a firm advertises its goods and services. The amount of money a business will have for its own uses will depend on the levels of taxation set by government.

THE JARGON DRAGON

pressure group – organisation that attempts to influence government and public opinion on a particular issue

Pressure groups

A <u>**pressure group**</u> is any group that has a particular point of view on a topic that it wants government or businesses to consider and support. Examples of pressure groups are Greenpeace, the organisation that campaigns over environmental issues (`www.greenpeace.org.uk`), and the Vegetarian Society (`www.Vegsoc.org`). Pressure groups are interested in persuading businesses to act in a way that reflects their point of view. They expect business leaders to listen to their opinions. Pressure groups can influence business by the research that they undertake in their area of interest and by creating publicity about the way a business is working.

Pressure groups find various ways of getting business or government to listen to their message

Suppliers

The people who supply the business with the things that it needs to carry out its activities are interested in the business being successful and placing more orders. They expect to be treated fairly and paid promptly. Suppliers can influence a business through the quality of what they supply. They can introduce new products or services and can affect the flow of production by the speed of their deliveries.

If a supplier delivers slowly the business they are sending the goods to may not be able to supply its customers and could lose income from sales. If a supplier is not happy with their customer the biggest impact they can have is to refuse to supply them.

Even the smallest business has many stakeholders and sometimes the interests of the stakeholders may conflict. Name as many examples as you can of stakeholders whose interests might conflict.

Think
IT THROUGH

case study

Actress joins call for Perrier boycott

Actress calls for Perrier award boycott

Well-known actress Emma Thompson is calling for a boycott of the Perrier Comedy Awards. The famous Oscar winner was responding to comedian Rob Newman's call to boycott the awards at the Edinburgh Fringe Festival because of Perrier's links to Nestlé, the food and sweets business.

'Nestlé has got to be stopped', said Thompson on Tuesday.

The boycott call is in protest at Nestlé's sale of powdered baby milk to developing countries. The protesters argue that breast-feeding should be encouraged as it is cheaper and reduces the risk of infection from contaminated water.

Nestlé points out that the way it promotes its products is in line with World Health Organisation guidelines.

'The accusations are out of date and our business behaviour has long since been changed', said Nestlé in London.

Pulp, Ocean Colour Scene, Richard E. Grant and Julie Walters have given their support to the pressure group Baby Milk Action, which campaigns on the issue. Baby Milk Action believe that if comedians support the

case study

Actress joins call for Perrier boycott

boycott and refuse to enter the famous comedy competition, they will succeed in getting Nestlé to change the way it does business in developing countries.

Based on BBC Website article October 2001 http://newssearch.bbc.co.uk

Q1 *In what ways could boycotts like the one described affect each of Nestlé's various stakeholders?*

Q2 *What sort of actions could Nestlé take to overcome the effects of the consumer boycott?*

Q3 *Is this sort of boycott justified?*

Financiers

These are the people who invest money in the business as part owners (see page 66) or who lend the business money (for example, banks). Financiers expect to make a profit on their loan or investment and for payments to be paid when they are due – so they are interested in the business doing well. Financiers can influence the business by changing the levels of interest they charge (see page 55) and through the amount they are prepared to invest.

Financiers provide the money that businesses need to operate

Look at the website of a major national newspaper for a story about how a business has had to deal with the interests of one or more of its stakeholders. Prepare a report for the class on what you found out.

Rights and responsibilities of employers and employees

Good working relationships are important to good team work and business success. When good working relationships are established the team works better. Punctuality, good attendance, pleasant manner of speaking and good attitude are all important in getting the trust of colleagues and employer. Employers can help by making sure employees have the materials and equipment they need to do their job. The best employers communicate with their employees so they feel informed about developments in the business. Safe and reasonably comfortable working conditions also help working relationships.

THE JARGON DRAGON

Intranet – run by companies and organisations as private networks for the benefit of their own staff

Communicating with employees

Firms use different ways to communicate with their employees in order to develop good working relationships.

- Larger firms will use their <u>intranet</u>, a staff newsletter and team meetings to give and receive information.
- In smaller firms word of mouth may be enough to communicate throughout the company and special efforts to communicate might not be needed.

Even in jobs when a person works alone he or she should be reliable. All members of the team need to be able to rely on each other to follow instructions, be punctual and attend work. If this doesn't happen the work will not be completed on time and customers and colleagues will be inconvenienced. Both customer relationships and working relations will suffer. The ability to follow instructions and be reliable is particularly important when matters of health and safety are concerned. For example, if you do not operate equipment according to the instructions you could injure yourself or someone else.

Investigating job roles

If everyone is clear about their roles and responsibilities and communication is good there is less chance of misunderstanding or confusion. This is made much easier if everyone has a **job description**. A job description also describes who the employee is responsible to and where he or she will work.

THE JARGON DRAGON

job description – a document listing all the tasks required to be done by someone in this post

PATRICK D. CALLAGHAN

WINE MERCHANT

JOB TITLE: RECEPTIONIST

1 To receive visitors to the company and to ensure that visitors sign the visitor's book when entering and leaving the building.

2 To operate the switchboard.

3 To undertake routine filing for the office manager.

4 To undertake routine typing for the office manager.

5 Any other reasonable duties that may from time to time be requested.

Reporting to: Head Receptionist

Date prepared: 8 September 2002

Organisation

An organisation chart is used in larger businesses to show where different jobs fit into the organisation.

An organisation chart

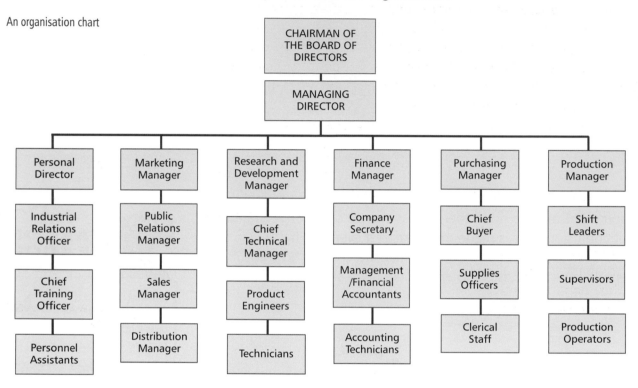

The organisation chart also shows the different levels of responsibility. People near the top have responsibility for those below them. From the diagram above you can see that the Managing Director is responsible for the whole business and reports to the Board of Directors. Different organisations will use different job titles, and sometimes job titles will vary within an organisation, as in the organisation chart shown here.

Below Director and Board level there are basically three levels of responsibility in a large to medium-sized organisation:

- manager
- supervisor
- operative.

These will be assisted by

- support staff.

The manager

A manager's key responsibilities are to ensure that his or her department meets its goals within its budget and according to the plans for the business (see page 5). A manager's activities include allocating work to people in their department and making sure it is done efficiently and on time. The manager will carry out the administrative tasks linked to these activities – e.g. preparing reports and writing letters. The manager has to make sure the department's staff are informed of developments in the business and that the directors know how the department is meeting its goals. In larger businesses a manager's job security will be linked to how well their department performs and the general economic performance of the business. Managers are involved in a wide range of decisions and have to solve problems to make sure that their department operates efficiently.

As well as having a good understanding of the business managers have to be able to deal well with people. It is rare for managers to be employed without qualifications at AS level equivalent or better (e.g. BTEC National Diploma, HND, Degree or Foundation Degree). Pay and **benefits** for managers are normally amongst the highest in the business. Benefits may include a company car, mobile phone and health insurance. However, if their department's performance is not good, the manager could be removed from their job.

THE JARGON DRAGON

benefits – rewards, other than pay, received by an employee

Managers' rewards are often linked to their performance

The supervisor

A supervisor is responsible for a group of staff within a department. The supervisor has a number of key responsibilities:

- making sure their team carries out the tasks given by the manager
- allocating work to people in their team

- planning operations to make sure tasks are done efficiently and on time
- preparing reports or filling in forms
- passing on information from the manager to the team
- making sure the manager is kept up to date with the progress of the team's work.

The supervisor's job security will be linked to how well their department performs and the performance of the business. He or she has a narrow range of decision-making powers but will be expected to solve problems so the team works efficiently and with good working relations. As well as having a thorough technical understanding of their work, supervisors are experienced operatives, usually having been promoted from this level. They will have good practical skills and should be able to get on with people.

Qualifications

Supervisors will have some qualifications, such as an NVQ Level Three or a supervisory qualification such as a NEBSM Certificate. These qualifications are not always necessary as some employers will appoint supervisors based on their personal qualities and experience. Generally speaking, qualifications do help when it comes to getting a supervisor's job.

Pay for supervisors will be higher than that for operatives, but they will not normally have the benefits that managers have. If

	Responsibilities	Activities	Job security	Decision making	Qualifications and personal qualities	Pay and benefits
Manager	Ensure department meets goals within budget	Allocate work to staff and ensure it is done efficiently and on time	Linked to departmental and business performance	Decides how particular tasks are allocated and carried out	Good with people; relevant qualifications at AS level or above	Highest paid employees in business; may include car and other benefits
Supervisor	For group of staff within department	Ensure tasks allocated by manager are completed as required	Linked to departmental and business performance	Decides how the team will tackle the jobs it has been given	Experienced in the work, practical skills; good at dealing with people	Not as well paid as managers; few if any benefits
Operative	To complete the work allocated on time and to a satisfactory standard	Practical activities to ensure sufficient output of good quality	Linked to departmental and business performance	Limited – operates within the guidelines of the firm	Reliable with good practical skills	Linked to hours worked and any bonus arrangements

Employees at all levels have better job security if the business is doing well

their team's performance is unsatisfactory a supervisor could lose their job.

The operative

Operatives are the people who actually produce the goods or services of the business. Their responsibilities are to ensure that they complete the tasks given to them on time and to a high standard. The operative will have few, if any, administrative tasks. He or she has to follow their supervisor's instructions and inform them if they have any problems in carrying out their tasks. The operative's job security will be linked to how well their department performs and the performance of the business.

An operative's decision-making powers are restricted to their duties and within a narrow set of guidelines laid down by the firm. Operatives need to have good practical skills. Some companies will help operatives gain qualifications linked to their job, such as NVQs – a chef might have NVQ Food Preparation (Level Two) while an office worker might have NVQ Administration (Level Two). Operatives will be paid a weekly wage linked to the hours they work.

If operatives work longer hours or meet performance targets they may qualify for an extra payment or bonus. For example, if a clothes machinist makes more than a certain number of garments in a week he or she might be paid extra.

Support staff

Support staff are the people who are not directly involved in producing goods or services for the business. Jobs can range from the very specialist tasks of research, marketing or accounting to gardening or cleaning the building. Their job security will be linked to the performance of the business – and in times of financial difficulty firms will tend to reduce their support staff before they reduce their production staff. The skills, decision making responsibilities and pay levels for support staff will vary according to the job undertaken.

Identify three staff roles in your school or college. Compare their responsibilities, activities, job security, decision making, qualifications and personal qualities needed for the job, pay and benefits.

FIND IT OUT

Working arrangements

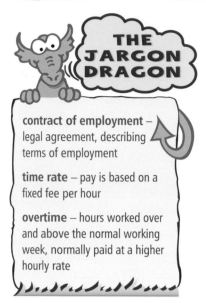

THE JARGON DRAGON

contract of employment – legal agreement, describing terms of employment

time rate – pay is based on a fixed fee per hour

overtime – hours worked over and above the normal working week, normally paid at a higher hourly rate

The legal relationship between employer and employee is written down in a **contract of employment**. This contract should be issued within 13 weeks of a person starting work. It must contain details of:

- rate of pay for the job in question, how it is calculated and any benefits
- hours to be worked
- place of work
- holiday entitlement
- sick pay arrangements
- length of notice to be worked
- job title
- whether the job is temporary or permanent.

Rate of pay

One of the most important parts of working is the pay. *Wages* are paid weekly and *salaries* are paid monthly. An employee's pay can be calculated in several ways.

Time rate

Time rate is a system that pays an employee according to the hours they work at so much per hour. The National Minimum Wage laws set down minimum hourly rates which adult workers must be paid (see page 95).

If an employee works more than the normal working week then he or she is paid at a higher hourly rate called **overtime**. For example, someone may be employed for a basic 35 hour week at £8.00 per hour. If he or she works more than 35 hours in the week (perhaps 3 hours overtime) he or she is paid at the overtime rate for those 3 hours. If the overtime rate is double time it means the employee receives double the hourly rate for the hours worked over the usual working week. In this example they will receive £16.00 per hour (double £8.00 per hour) for their 3 hours overtime – a total overtime pay of £48.00. Instead of paying overtime some firms have a system of giving staff time off work equal to the amount of overtime worked. This is known as time off in lieu.

Organisations which have a time rate system have a method of recording the hours worked. This may involve clocking in, where a time-keeping machine stamps the time on an employee's clocking in card, or signing in a book to show the time of arrival and departure from work. As the time rate system pays employees for the hours they work there is no financial encouragement for them to produce work quickly or to a higher standard. This lack of incentive or encouragement is a disadvantage from the employer's point of view. Sometimes a bonus is used in the time rate system to encourage hourly paid workers to meet production targets, This is intended to overcome the lack of incentive to produce at maximum output. An advantage of the system is that it is fairly simple and cheap to operate.

Piece rate

Under a **piece rate** system workers are paid for each piece of work they do. For example, machinists in a factory producing shirts will be paid for each shirt they make to an acceptable standard. As long as the employee meets minimum standards of output (e.g. a minimum number of shirts to an acceptable standard each day), the amount of time taken is less important. Piece rate systems are designed to encourage employees to produce as much as possible in the time available and so overcome some of the problems of the time rate system. It is more complicated to organise as each worker's output has to be monitored to ensure that their work is of an acceptable standard and that each worker is paid in relation to what they produce.

THE JARGON DRAGON

piece rate – payment based on a worker's output

This machinist will be paid for each shirt she makes to an acceptable standard

THE JARGON DRAGON

bonus – additional payment for meeting certain business requirements

commission – payment that is related to the value of sales made

It is not uncommon under this system to pay workers a **bonus** if they produce more than certain target levels. Bonus payments are higher than the basic piece rate and are intended to encourage the employees to exceed their targets. The employer benefits because output is higher. A disadvantage is that rushing production to reach a bonus payment may reduce quality, produce unacceptable items and waste materials.

Commission

A group of people do not receive payment according to time rate. If you have a friend or relative who runs a catalogue such as Avon Cosmetics or Betterware you may have heard them talk of the **commission** they receive. The commission is their payment for selling goods. The amount of commission is worked out according to the value of the goods sold. A commission of 10% means that the person selling the catalogue goods receives 10% of the value of the sales they make. For example, if they sell something for £10.00 they will receive £1.00 commission. Insurance salespeople are often paid commission on the value of the financial services they sell. Individuals who work on a commission-only basis like this are similar to piece-rate workers – what they earn depends on how successful they are. From an employer's point of view commission-only systems encourage hard work, while the employee has the prospect of unlimited earnings – if he or she is successful! Commission payments have to be carefully monitored in order to ensure that each employee is receiving the correct payment.

Lots of goods are sold on commission

Tupperware
Making it all possible

catalogue 1-2002

It is common for sales staff to be paid commission on their sales

Mixed systems

It is not unusual to find organisations using combinations of the payment systems we have looked at. For example, employees in a department store could be paid on a time rate basis but also receive commission on the sales they make. The percentage commission will be less than someone working on a commission-only basis because he or she will receive an hourly income as well. In certain industries employers use a combination of time rate and piece work.

Benefits

In addition to being paid an employee may be offered other benefits by their employer. These extra rewards for employees in addition to the pay and bonuses they receive are known as <u>fringe benefits</u> or perks. Common benefits include staff canteen, company car, luncheon vouchers, sports or recreation facilities, discount on purchases of the firm's goods, medical insurance and opportunities to buy shares in the firm at a reduced price. In some cases employees have to have been employed by the firm for a certain length of time before they qualify for fringe benefits – for example, bank employees may have to be with the bank for a minimum of one year before being allowed to borrow money at a reduced rate of interest.

THE JARGON DRAGON

fringe benefits – non-pay rewards to employees, e.g. a company car

Pay can be calculated in several ways – some employees may get fringe benefits and a bonus

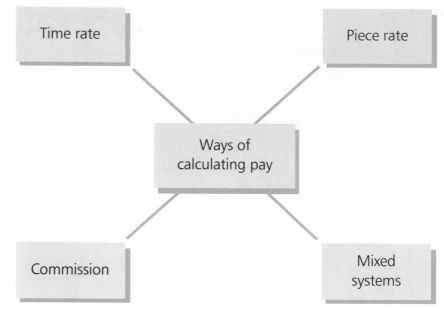

Time rate

Piece rate

Ways of calculating pay

Commission

Mixed systems

THE JARGON DRAGON

PAYE – Pay As You Earn – method of paying tax in instalments, based on the previous year's income and personal circumstances

The employer is required to deduct income tax from the employee's pay under the Pay As You Earn (**PAYE**) system. The amount a person pays is linked to how much they earn and their family and financial circumstances. This system, based on the previous year's income, avoids the employee having to pay tax in a lump sum each year, and tax is paid in instalments during the year. The amount of tax to be paid is shown by the employee's tax code, which shows how much they are allowed to earn before paying tax. Just after the end of each tax year (5th April) the employee receives a P60 form from the Inland Revenue, which shows how much tax has been deducted and the total amount their employer has paid them over the year. This should

The P60 form shows how much tax an employee has paid over the year

P60 for Tax Year 2002-03

The illustration below is actual A4 size.

Single-part, short version

Suitable for completion manually or by sheet-feed printer.

P60 End of Year Certificate

Tax Year to 5 April 2003

To the employee:

Please keep this certificate in a safe place as you will not be able to get a duplicate. **You will need it if you have to fill in a Tax Return.**

You can also use it to check that your employer is deducting the right rate of National Insurance contributions for you and using your correct National Insurance number.

By law you are required to tell the Inland Revenue about any income that is not fully taxed, even if you are not sent a Tax Return.

INLAND REVENUE

Employee's details

Surname

Forenames or initials

National Insurance number   Works/payroll number

Pay and Income Tax details

	Pay £ p	Tax deducted £ p
In previous employment(s)		
In this employment	Pay	Tax deducted If refund mark 'R'

Figures shown here should be used for your Tax Return, if you get one   Final tax code

Employee's Widows & Orphans/Life Assurance contributions in this employment   £ p

National Insurance contributions in this employment

be carefully checked, in case there has been a miscalculation and too much or too little tax has been paid. Certain benefits, such as a company car, are taxable.

Hours of work

These are an important consideration when starting a new job. Most companies will lay down the starting and finishing times of the job (e.g. 8:30 am to 4:30 pm with tea and lunch breaks at fixed times), but more and more are moving to a system of flexitime. Flexitime means 'flexible time'. Most flexitime systems require workers to be in work between certain times, such as between 10:30 am and 3:00 pm. This fixed time is called the core time. As long as an employee is at work during the core time they can start and finish more or less when they please – provided they complete the required number of hours per week or month.

From an employee's point of view this system has many attractions. Being able to start and finish work as you wish allows more freedom in your personal life – for instance, to collect children from school, attend meetings or go shopping. Most flexitime systems allow employees to work more than the required hours in a particular week or month and have the time off in lieu at a later date (see page 78). This increases the individual's control over their life. If an employee works fewer than the required hours he or she must make up the time during the following week or month. Although flexitime can be difficult to organise from an employer's point of view it can lead to a happier work force who are working more efficiently at the times that suit them best.

Jobs such as clerical work, which involves limited contact with the public and other workers, are well suited to the system. Jobs that involve regular daily contact with other people, like teaching, could not be done efficiently under a flexitime system – for instance, pupils would not be certain when teachers were available to teach them.

Manufacturing industries commonly use a shift system of working. This means one team of workers starts work as another finishes. Using equipment more or less continuously is more cost-effective from the firm's point of view. Shift work gives employees free time during the day but some people find working night shifts unpleasant. An unsocial hours payment is often made for shifts done outside the normal working day. Night work in a factory would usually qualify for such a payment.

THE JARGON DRAGON

flexitime – an arrangement of flexible working hours

core time – set working hours within flexitime arrangements

cost-effective – activity that has desired results at a reasonable cost

Place of work

The contract will indicate the employee's main place of work. This might be an office, retail outlet such as a shop, or call centre for tele-sales. The employee may be mobile or work from home. Even contracts that indicate a place of work will often have a paragraph which gives the firm the right to change the place of work if business needs require it.

All employees are entitled to a minimum of 20 days holiday per year

Holiday arrangements

The contract will indicate how many days leave the employee is entitled to take each year. Some firms will allow a few days' holiday to be carried over into the following year. Employees will not be able to take the holidays they want without first checking with their manager or supervisor that the business will not be disrupted if they go on leave as planned. Most full-time employees are entitled to a minimum of 20 days per year in addition to Bank Holidays such as Easter Monday or New Year's Day. In a lot of jobs holiday entitlement increases with each year of employment with that employer, to a maximum of between 25 and 38 days.

Arrangements for sick pay

If you are unable to work because you are ill you may still be entitled to pay. Your contract will describe what you have to do to claim sick pay.

THE JARGON DRAGON

notice period – period of time a person has to work between handing in their resignation and leaving their job

Length of notice

Most contracts will say that once you have told the firm you wish to leave, or if they ask you to leave, you will still have to work for a certain period of time before you go. This allows the company time to find a replacement, or you to find a new job. This period of time is the **notice period**. The notice period will vary according the job and the employer but is normally a week or a month.

Working more flexibly

The contract of employment sets out the basic entitlements of employer and employee. However, business conditions can become more difficult or new business opportunities may arise once you have started your job. Your employer might wish to introduce changes that require you to be more flexible. There are many reasons for more flexible working.

Increasing productivity

Increased productivity means producing more by not increasing costs, or at least increasing them by less than the increase in production. Changes in working hours or payment rates can help increase productivity. For example, if production increases by 20% but costs rise by only 10% this is an increase in productivity. If working hours increase by 10% and the firm's output rises by 15% this is also an increase in productivity.

Improving the quality of products

Better quality products can lead to increased sales and business success. For example, asking quality control staff to move from a 9:00 am to 5:00 pm working day on a five-day week to shifts spread over seven days could make them available to check quality and correct errors before production has gone too far.

Being more competitive

Firms can improve their competitiveness in many ways, for example by improving delivery time or by lowering prices. Increased competitiveness can mean changes in working practices such as changing working hours to suit customers' needs. For instance, the hours of delivery drivers might be changed so that deliveries could be made at weekends and evenings – they would still work the same number of hours but would help to make the firm more competitive.

Introducing new technology

New technology can help competitiveness, for example, by reducing errors or speeding up production. The use of new technology may require further training by the employee or a new pay system to reflect the changes the new technology has made to working arrangements (see page 30).

Introducing team-working and multi-skill practices

This means sharing work through a team and having the team members develop skills in more than one task. This often improves productivity and competitiveness. It may involve staff retraining or moving the place of work to premises more suited to the new approaches. For example, Volvo cars uses a team-work approach, where employees discuss problems and solve them by working on a number of different tasks. Some other car manufacturers have their employees concentrating on only one task and being told what to do by their supervisor.

Rights of employers and employees

Employers' rights

Employers expect their employees to:

- meet the terms of their contract
- co-operate in meeting the objectives of the business and
- follow Health and Safety regulations.

Meeting the terms of the contract

Complying with your contract means that you have to follow the agreements in your contract of employment. For example, you should start and finish work at the times stated in your contract, you should only take the number of days holiday to which you are entitled. This entitlement is described in your contract.

If you are ill you must report this to your employer and present a <u>sick note</u>. For an absence of up to five days you are allowed to complete a sick note yourself. This is known as self-certification. After five days you must have your sick note completed by a doctor.

THE JARGON DRAGON

sick note – official document confirming employee illness

If you are unhappy about any aspects of your job there is a system for making this known. This is called a grievance procedure. Usually you should discuss problems with your supervisor first. If this does not improve things your trade union can provide advice and represent your views to your employer.

If you break your contract of employment you are not complying with it. Examples of this would be taking days off work that you are not entitled to (poor attendance), starting work late (poor punctuality) or leaving early without permission. Not following instructions from your employer or supervisor is also non-compliance with your contract. If you do not meet the terms of your contract disciplinary action could be taken against you, and you could eventually be dismissed.

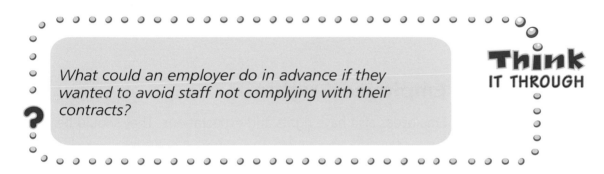

What could an employer do in advance if they wanted to avoid staff not complying with their contracts?

Think
IT THROUGH

Co-operating in meeting the objectives of the business

Most businesses will try to be clear about what their objectives are and communicate these to their employees. You will be expected to co-operate in meeting these objectives by being flexible in your working.

Following health and safety regulations

The Health and Safety at Work Act 1974 requires all employees to co-operate with employers in working safely. This means that you must follow safety regulations and wear protective clothes, hats, boots or goggles if they are needed. All employees must observe 'no smoking' regulations and follow the rules that limit where and when you are allowed to smoke on work premises. Under the law, you must also take reasonable steps to protect yourself and others in the work you do. This means you should not take any safety risks in carrying out your duties.

Employees should always follow safety regulations and wear protective clothing if required

Employees' rights

Employees also have rights and expectations. They should be:

- paid according to their contract
- provided with a safe working environment
- appropriately trained
- permitted to join trade unions or staff associations (see page 89) and
- allowed access to any confidential computer records kept on them as employees.

Payment according to contract

It is in everyone's interest that the contract of employment is as clear as possible about pay. Agreement on levels of pay and prompt payment keep the workforce happy. On page 100 we look at what happens if disagreements arise.

Providing a safe working environment

Just as employees are expected to work safely, employers are legally obliged to provide a working environment that is safe. We will consider this more fully on page 96.

Look in a local or national newspaper for any reports about accidents at work. Summarise the report by saying how the accident(s) happened and what actions followed.

Appropriate training

Workers who want to work flexibly and help the business develop will expect to be trained by the employer so that they can do this. Suitable training not only helps a person do the job they are paid for but often prepares them to move to different and better paid work.

Permitted to join trade unions or staff associations

Although employer and employee relations are generally good, millions of employees belong to a trade union in case the relationship breaks down. Teachers might belong to the NUT (National Union of Teachers), while journalists could join the NUJ (National Union of Journalists). Trade unions can represent their members to the employer, negotiate on their behalf and offer legal advice. Wage negotiations between an employer and a trade union on behalf of its members are common. A number of trade unions offer other services such as low cost insurance or a credit card. Staff associations are similar to a trade union but generally restrict their representation to one employer, unlike a trade union that will have members with different employers. Unions generally belong to the TUC (Trades Union Congress), staff associations do not.

THE JARGON DRAGON

TUC – Trades Union Congress – organisation that represents trade unions

The TUC holds a general conference every year

Allowing access to confidential information

Sometimes people feel unhappy if their employer holds records about them that they are not allowed to see. Under the Data Protection Act employees are entitled to have access to computer records about themselves and the way the computer stored information can be used is limited.

Employees and employers should meet each other's expectations

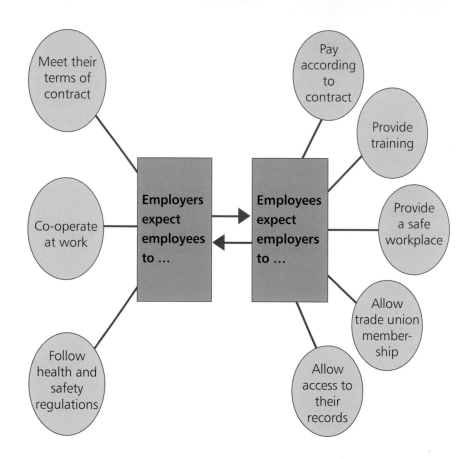

Protecting rights

The rights of employer and employee are protected by laws in several important areas.

- Equal pay
- Discrimination linked to disability, gender and race
- Employment rights and working hours
- Health and safety
- Access to information

Equal pay

The Sex Discrimination Act 1975 established that it is not legal to pay men and women different rates of pay if they are doing work of a similar nature. This Act states that people must be treated equally in other ways too, for example promotion and training opportunities.

Discrimination

In most situations discrimination linked to disability, gender or race is illegal. To support employers and employees the government has established several organisations to ensure that the law is implemented fairly.

Disability

The Disability Rights Commission (DRC) was established to work with disabled people to ensure they are treated fairly. The DRC was set up under the Disability Discrimination Act 1995. This law is intended to stop discrimination against disabled people. This includes recruitment, training and benefits. The DRC oversees the law, and in particular

- stops discrimination against disabled people
- promotes equal opportunities for disabled people
- provides information and advice to disabled people, employers and service providers
- prepares **codes of practice** and encourages good practice
- investigates discrimination and makes sure the law is implemented.

THE JARGON DRAGON

code of practice – written guidelines on good business procedures

Disabled people who feel they have been unfairly treated can ask the DRC to investigate their case. However, the act does not apply to all jobs – there are exceptions:

- small businesses with fewer than 15 employees
- employment on ships, aircraft and hovercraft
- people in the armed services, police officers, prison officers and fire fighting staff in fire brigades.

case study

Racism gets worse in Britain's workplaces

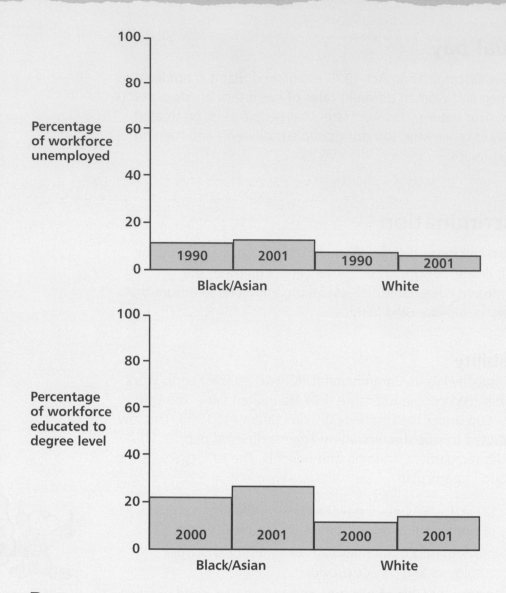

Percentage of workforce unemployed

Percentage of workforce educated to degree level

Racism in Britain's workplaces is intensifying as Black and Asian people are now more than twice as likely to be unemployed as their White counterparts, says a new TUC report, *Black workers deserve better*.

Black and Asian joblessness today stands at 12%, while among White people it is just 5%. This position is worse than in 1990, when Black and Asian unemployment was lower, at 11%, and higher among the White population (6%). This trend has grown worse despite unemployment dropping. Black and Asian workers have clearly not gained equally from Britain's expanding economy compared with their White counterparts.

John Monks, TUC General Secretary, said: 'Too many employers are ignoring the lessons of the MacPherson Inquiry into the murder of Stephen Lawrence. They have to face up to the reality of racism in their organisations and act against it. Despite unemployment dropping below one million our Black and Asian workers are still suffering discrimination.

'And this is made worse as Black and Asian workers are passed over for managerial jobs, even though they have skilled themselves by gaining more higher educational qualifications. All employers should monitor their recruitment and promotion procedures and reverse this unacceptable position.'

In some of Britain's regions the situation is even worse. In both Yorkshire and Humberside and the West Midlands 5% of White workers are unemployed, compared with 15% of Blacks and Asians. But even after getting a job Black and Asian workers still face discrimination as they find it increasingly difficult to get managerial posts. And this occurs despite Black workers making serious efforts to equip themselves for promotion. The proportion of black and Asian workers educated to degree level or above increased from 21% to 26% over the last 18 months. In the same period White employees with similar qualifications increased only from 16% to 17%.

Based on an article from the TUC Website http://www.tuc.org.uk/
27 April 2001.

Q1 *How have the proportions of Black and White workers with degrees or high qualifications changed in the 18 months before this report? At the time this report was published, what was the unemployment rate for Black and Asian workers compared with that for White workers?*

Q2 *Where could an employer who wanted advice about avoiding racial discrimination find that advice?*

Q3 *If a business ignores well-qualified Black and Asian employees how could this affect its performance?*

Look at **www.disability.gov.uk** *for information about government efforts to help disabled people. Write a summary of what is being done.*

Gender

The aim of the Equal Opportunities Commission (EOC) is to ensure that people are not treated less favourably because of their sex. The Sex Discrimination Act 1975 makes it illegal to treat one person more favourably than another on the grounds of their sex. Job advertisements can only ask for a specific sex if there is a genuine reason (or genuine occupational qualification as it is called). Acceptable reasons might include the fact that a woman is needed to supervise a residential home for the female elderly or that a man is required to model male clothes. In other words, only reasons of decency or where features typical of only one sex are required allow an employer to discriminate against one sex. It is illegal to discriminate on the grounds that customers prefer staff of one sex. For example, pubs and clubs can no longer legally advertise for bar *maids*.

If someone believes they have been discriminated against on the grounds of their sex they can seek help from a trade union, solicitor, Citizen's Advice Bureau or the EOC.

The EOC can provide advice and information to help prevent disputes over equal opportunities. It has produced a number of codes of practice, which are guidelines for dealing with particular equal opportunities situations. The EOC may help employees who feel discriminated against to take their employer to court or an employment tribunal. An employment tribunal operates like a court and has legal powers to decide the outcome of employment related disputes. If it suspects discrimination is taking place the EOC may issue a non-discriminatory notice against the employer to warn them to improve the situation or face further legal action.

Race

The Race Relations Act 1976 made it illegal to treat one person less favourably than another in employment on the grounds of their race, nationality, colour or ethnic group. This covers all aspects of employment including training, promotion, recruitment or conditions of service. The Commission for Racial

Equality (CRE) was established to ensure that the aims of the Act are met. To help prevent disputes over racial matters, the CRE can provide advice and information to employers and employees. Its codes of practice are guidelines for dealing with particular situations where racial discrimination might occur. In certain circumstances the CRE (Commission for Racial Equality) may help employees who feel discriminated against to take the employer to court or an employment tribunal. If it suspects discrimination is taking place the CRE may issue a non-discrimination notice against the employer. This is a legal document warning the employer to improve the situation or face further legal action.

Look at the website for the Equal Opportunities Commission (www.eoc.org.uk) and the Commission for Racial Equality (www.cre.gov.uk). Describe the ways in which the work of each organisation is similar and different.

Employment rights and working hours

The Employment Relations Act 1999

The Employment Relations Act 1999 lays down the conditions in which employers have to recognise and negotiate with a trade union. It is illegal for employers to discriminate against employees on the grounds that they are trade union members. Workers who prove in an employment tribunal that they have been unfairly dismissed may be compensated up to £50 000. The act also allows mothers and fathers limited time off for child care or family reasons.

The Working Time Regulations

The Working Time Regulations give employees the right not to work more than 48 hours a week unless they agree to do so in writing. The same regulations allow a minimum of 11 hours off between each working day, with 12 hours for workers under 18 years of age. Adult workers are entitled to one day off per week and under 18s to two days off, or 36 hours in exceptional circumstances.

The National Minimum Wage

All adult workers over 18 are entitled to the National Minimum Wage, which is the minimum employers must pay. The rate increases after the age of 21 but people under 18 do not qualify. The National

Minimum Wage is set by the government annually and for most of 2002 the figure was £4.10 per hour. The rate is reconsidered by the government in October of each year. An employee cannot be dismissed for asking to be paid the National Minimum Wage. Employees are not allowed to sign away their right to the minimum wage. Employers are required by law to keep records that show all employees are being paid the minimum wage and must show these records to an employee if he or she asks to see them. A firm can be fined up to £50 000 for not paying the National Minimum Wage.

Think
IT THROUGH

What are the practical advantages and disadvantages of the National Minimum Wage and Working Time Regulations from an employer's and employee's point of view?

?

Health and safety

The law requires employers to provide a safe working environment and employees to co-operate in working safely.

Health and Safety at Work Act 1974

Under this law employers have a duty to make sure that the workplace is safe and does not in any way harm the health of employees, customers or visitors. Employees have a legal duty to co-operate with their employer in making the workplace safe. They also have to ensure that anything they do does not put the health of other employees at risk. All the people working in an organisation have a responsibility to make sure visitors and customers are not put at risk.

The working of the Health and Safety at Work Act (HSWA) is overseen by the Health and Safety Executive (HSE), which provides information and advice about safe working. The HSE is also responsible for enforcing the Working Time Regulations (see page 95). The HSE produces a series of booklets and leaflets for employers and employees covering a range of health and safety issues. An important publication is the *Essentials of Health and Safety at Work* booklet, which provides much helpful information about safety in the workplace. The HSE also arranges for the inspection of premises if there is concern about the safety of workers or customers.

Control of Substances Hazardous to Health 1988 (COSHH)

These regulations are known as the COSHH regulations. They require employers to carry out an assessment of the risks caused by all chemicals, materials and other substances used in the workplace. If substances that may be hazardous to health are being used the employer must make sure that clear rules for the use and storage of these materials are followed so that risk is reduced to the absolute minimum. Employees must co-operate with the safety procedures introduced by the employer.

Management of Health and Safety at Work Regulations 1992

These regulations are sometimes called the Framework Directive because they bring together previous laws and regulations and put them into a set of rules approved by the European Union. They add to the other regulations described above by covering matters such as lifting objects, evacuation procedures, drinking water and first-aid equipment. Employers must provide free to their employees protective clothes and equipment that meet European Union regulations and standards. The regulations also describe protective measures for people using computers and word processors for long periods of time.

Access to information

People's access to information about themselves is controlled by the 1998 Data Protection Act. The workings of the Act are monitored by the Information Commissioner. The Act states that anyone holding information about an individual must register this fact with the Commissioner and follow the code of conduct. Organisations can only hold sensitive information about a person, such as their ethnic origin, political opinions or trade union membership, with that individual's permission. The law applies to both computer records and paper records.

Organisations holding the information about a person must allow that person to see it within 40 days of their request to see it. Information holders are allowed to charge a small fee to cover administrative costs. Disputes about the Act are dealt with by the

Information Commissioner. Directors of businesses can be fined £5000 or more if they or their employees break this law.

These are some of the organisations that can advise about employer and employee rights

Under the National Minimum Wage regulations employees can request to see records that show they are being paid the minimum wage. Employers who refuse may be fined.

Visit **www.dataprotection.gov.uk** *and find the name of the Information Commissioner. List the eight enforceable principles of good practice. Discuss how they might affect the practical work of a business.*

Resolving disagreements

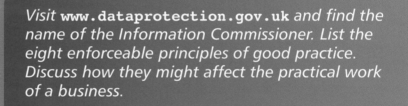

As businesses change and develop to meet customer needs and economic conditions, sometimes disagreements arise about the treatment of individual employees or groups of employees. For example, attempts to make a business more flexible by changing working hours or pay levels can cause disagreements if they are not handled properly. There are several ways disagreements can be resolved.

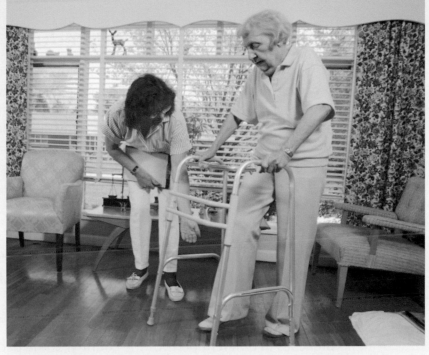

A care worker who was injured after slipping on wet laundry and had to give up work as a result has been awarded more than £200 000 compensation after UNISON took up her case. The payout comes after bosses at Newcastle City Council at first offered her just £9,500 in damages. Residential home carer Karen Martin, aged 37 when the incident occurred, was carrying dirty clothes to a washing machine when she slipped at Riverside View Residential Home in Byker, Newcastle upon Tyne. Her former employer argued that Mrs Martin had a pre-existing back complaint that would have stopped her working within a year of the accident in any case. UNISON's head of health and safety Hugh Robertson said: 'This is a tragic case, and one that could have been easily avoided if the employer had simply followed the manual handling regulations. However, while compensation can never recompense the lives destroyed by back injury, it does show that workers need trade union advice and support to get their due entitlement from their employer.'

Briefing from TUC Website http://www.tuc.org.uk

Q1 *How can employers prevent incidents like this one occurring?*

Q2 *How can employees protect themselves from these sort of incidents?*

Business grievance procedure

Employers normally agree with the trade unions a set of procedures about how to settle a disagreement between employees or between employees and the management. These procedures will vary from firm to firm but will usually involve independent representatives of the people concerned considering the complaint and coming to a decision. Employees are allowed to have representatives with them during the process.

Negotiations with trade unions or other representative organisations

To make sure their views are represented employees will often join a trade union. These are national organisations with branches in different parts of the country. Some people choose to join a staff association, whose activities are restricted to a particular employer. In both cases negotiations about disputes at a workplace (or plant) level are carried out between local representatives (in a union these are called shop stewards) and the employer's representatives. Local or plant discussions often deal with piece rates, bonus payments, staff facilities and health and safety matters.

Such discussions are known as **collective bargaining** because the representatives of employers and unions are speaking on behalf of their collection of members, who will respect the outcome of the discussions. Most disagreements are settled by this sort of negotiation. When disagreements cannot be settled in this way

THE JARGON DRAGON

collective bargaining – negotiations about working conditions between representatives of employers and representatives of unions

Negotiations about workplace disputes usually involve union shop stewards and representatives of the employer

they are said to be deadlocked. The trade unions might then take various sorts of industrial action to support their case. These include strikes (refusing to work), working to rule (strictly following rules so that work is disrupted) or a go slow (working very slowly).

> *The TUC is an organisation of over 70 trade unions. At* **www.tuc.org.uk/tuc/unions_main.cfm** *there is a description of how to choose a union that is best for you along with a list of unions.*
> 1 *Before you visit the site pick three jobs that you or your friends think might suit you when you start work.*
> 2 *Choose from the list of over 70 unions on the website which union would be right for you.*
> 3 *How you could find more information if you are not sure which is best?*

FIND IT OUT

Employment tribunals

These are often known as industrial tribunals, and have been set up by parliament to resolve disputes over matters of employment. Over 100 000 complaints a year are referred to an employment tribunal. They deal with things such as unfair dismissal, redundancy payments and disputes about the Working Time Regulations. Tribunals are chaired by an independent, legally qualified, person appointed by the government. There are two other members of the tribunal who are nominated by trade unions and employers. These people consider cases put before them and give a verdict. Employment tribunals are less formal in their approach than a court of law. If the employer or employee disagrees with the tribunal's interpretation of the law they can appeal to an Employment appeal tribunal.

Arbitration services

There a number of services that will arbitrate (decide) on a dispute between employers and employees. Having an outsider decide on a disagreement often avoids the need for industrial action. The Advisory, Conciliation and Arbitration Service (ACAS) is the most well known arbitration service. The aim of ACAS is to improve **industrial relations**.

THE JARGON DRAGON

industrial relations – system of negotiation between employers and employees

ACAS has 800 staff in 11 regional centres across England, Scotland and Wales who try to help businesses avoid disputes before they arise. ACAS helps in four ways.

Impartial information and help

Over 760,000 calls are made each year to the ACAS helplines about a range of employment-related disputes and questions. ACAS also produce a range of publications, many of them on their website (`www.acas.org.uk`).

Preventing and resolving problems

Hundreds of companies each year use ACAS to work with them and employee representatives to resolve problems. The advisory service of ACAS works with firms to prevent disputes arising by sharing good practices used in other similar organisations.

Settling complaints about employees' rights

Over 100,000 complaints a year are referred to an employment tribunal, but before they go that far most of them are referred to ACAS to see if they can be resolved. Over 70% of complaints are resolved before they have to go to an employment tribunal.

Encouraging people to work together effectively

ACAS runs courses on employment-related matters and changes in employment laws. The events are publicised on their website.

ACAS exists to improve industrial relations

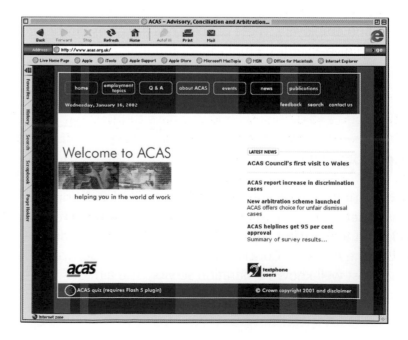

The European Court of Justice

This ensures that the law relating to the various agreements between the member states of the European Union are observed. These agreements or treaties deal with employment related matters. In certain situations an individual may take a complaint to this court, and financial help is sometimes available to do this, depending on the individual's circumstances.

The European Court of Justice is made up of 15 judges from the member states of the European Union, supported by eight Advocates General.

Recruitment and training

To be successful a business needs employees who have the right skills and attitudes. When recruiting staff the managers need to be aware of their legal obligations. They also need to decide whether to develop the skill of an existing member of staff or recruit from outside.

You will soon be making decisions about what job you would like to do. In making your decision about what sort of job to go for you should consider how suitable it is to you.

Sometimes people are attracted to a particular job title or company. You have to know yourself – your own ideas, background and opinions – and you have to investigate the job before you decide what to do. Everyone's ideas are influenced by their friends and relatives. Deciding on your first job can affect the rest of your life. Because this is so important you need to be sure that the decision you make is the one that suits you best. It means you have to be honest with yourself about what you want and what you are like. You should carefully consider several factors.

case study

Making it your business to be a success

Schools are breaking up this week for the summer holidays. For many students there will be an anxious wait for A-level and GCSE results. I would like to persuade you that business can provide a rewarding and challenging career and to emphasise how important it is to have the right skills.

The pace of economic change has left regions like ours facing a big challenge. Manufacturing industry only provides about a quarter of our wealth now. We need all of you who are planning your futures to consider a career in business. There is such a choice – engineering, marketing, accountancy, computing, personnel – and improving skills and lifelong learning will be absolutely fundamental in achieving this.

Technological change is increasing our ability to automate away low-skilled jobs. It is also helping to create new areas of the economy where the product is not something made, but is information – the intellectual property rights, the design, the software. Just think, no one had heard of website design seven or eight years ago. Now it is a major industry.

New work practices mean more flexible individuals and teams, and an emphasis on multi-skilling – having a number of skills you can use in the workplace. So the buzzword now is 'employability' – having the right skills to meet the changing needs of employers. A lot of this falls on the individual. No one else can manage your career for you and no one else can learn for you.

Employers are going to be looking for more young people with good communication skills, who can be self-starters with good self-discipline, and who can work as a team.

However well you do at school academically you will not fulfil your potential in life without several very important qualities. The first is consistency of purpose, or determination. The second is a sense of urgency, having a 'do it now' philosophy. I can think of a number of people who have turned limited success at school into great success in life with these qualities. Always having a positive attitude to life helps enormously. We need bright young people to look for careers in business because we need to transform the economies of regions like ours.

Based on an article in the *Yorkshire Evening Post*, July 2001, by CBI Regional Director Penny Hemming

Q1 *Explain the phrase 'automate away low-skilled jobs'. How does this affect school leavers?*

Q2 *What positive effects does new technology have on job opportunities?*

Q3 *Apart from qualifications, what qualities do employers look for in young people?*

Your circumstances

Practical issues like how easy it is to travel to work, and how much it costs, are among the things you should be thinking about. It shouldn't take up too much of your time or wages to get to work. If you can find suitable accommodation near the job you want this might solve the problem.

Some jobs may affect your health if you have allergies or other problems. For example, if you are allergic to cats you would probably not be happy working in a veterinary surgery. People with sensitive skin would be unlikely to find a career in hairdressing rewarding if their skin was affected by chemicals. A hay fever sufferer would be unhappy as a gardener or florist.

THE JARGON DRAGON

unsocial hours – jobs that require you to work outside normal office hours

If you have to care for a child or relative the hours you are available for work might be limited so you would have to avoid jobs that have **unsocial hours**. People receiving state benefits should consider the effect of taking particular jobs on their entitlement to benefits. If there is likely to be a problem speak to your benefits office or advisers in college, at school or in organisations such as the Citizens' Advice Bureau (CAB).

Some jobs may affect your health if you have allergies or other problems

Your qualifications

Are the qualifications you have or are likely to achieve suitable to get you the job you want? Many jobs will require academic qualifications such as GCSEs, A levels, AVCEs and AS or vocational qualifications such as an NVQ or BTEC National Award. If you don't have the qualifications needed for the job you should either consider an alternative job or do further study to get the qualifications you need. Your teachers or lecturers will advise you about your academic progress.

Your interests

You are more likely to be better or happier doing something you are interested in. Try to find jobs that use your interests – animals, computers, photography, being outdoors, using equipment, maths, music, meeting people, etc. But take care when considering this, as many of your interests and hobbies may be because you took them up with friends and family. You should ask yourself if you are really interested enough in doing this for years to come. You have to be prepared to accept that all jobs have aspects to them which are less interesting than you would like but your choice of job should keep this to a minimum.

Available opportunities

In choosing the sort of work you want you need to fix your sights on jobs that are reasonably available to you. For example, you should look at positions that are suitable as your first job rather than at ones that require lots of experience or qualifications you do not yet have. However, do not set your sights too low.

The job you choose should offer further progression in the sector of business you have chosen. You need to look at jobs carefully to see what the opportunities are for future progression. A job might look attractive in terms of what you do and the pay level but you need to ask yourself how attractive these things will be in the future if you have not progressed.

Look at the situations vacant in your local newspaper. Find three jobs you might be interested in and by using a library or searching on the internet get more information about them. Assess how well suited you are to those posts.

FIND IT OUT

Recruitment

There are eight stages involved in recruitment of staff. You should know about these so you can make the best possible applications for work.

- Identifying the vacancy
- Drawing up a job specification
- Drawing up a person specification
- Advertising the vacancy
- Drawing up a shortlist
- Interviewing applicants
- Selecting the most suitable candidate
- Offering the job and agreeing the conditions.

Identifying the vacancy

Before a firm fills a vacancy it has to make sure that it needs to fill it. For a new post the firm will have to consider if it should move existing staff around or retrain them. For a replacement post new, more advanced, equipment might mean that individuals with different qualifications to the previous employee are needed. If there have been improvements in efficiency the post can be left unfilled without affecting production. Perhaps a part-time appointment will be sufficient. This means that the person is employed for only part of the working week, and paid accordingly. A full-time employee works for the full working week. Once the evaluation is complete, the recruitment process can start.

THE JARGON DRAGON

job description – a document listing all the tasks required to be done by someone in this post

Drawing up a job description

A list of the main duties will be prepared along with other information, such as to whom the post holder will be responsible and where they will work. This **job description** can take many different forms, according to the type of job and the firm concerned. Job descriptions can be written using information obtained from the previous employee, the manager or supervisor who know about the duties and using direct observation of the job in question.

Drawing up a person specification

The Personnel Department (or Human Resources Department) will help to identify what sort of skills, qualifications and experience are required in order for the job to be done well. This <u>person specification</u> is used to judge the suitability of applicants during the process of selection. A specification for a typist might require that applicants can type at 45 words per minute while a requirement for a hotel porter might be that they have good health and can lift heavy objects. A hotel manager might be required to have an HND or degree in Hospitality Management.

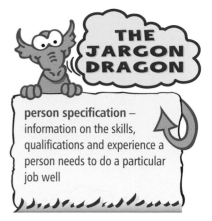

THE JARGON DRAGON

person specification – information on the skills, qualifications and experience a person needs to do a particular job well

Advertising the vacancy

Newspaper advertisements, employment agencies, Job Centres and school or college careers services are all ways in which firms can draw the attention of members of the public to its vacancies. In some cases – such as for posts above the firm's basic pay grades – people already working for the firm might be encouraged to apply or the position is advertised only inside the firm. This is called internal advertising. Most vacancies are advertised in newspapers or magazines.

The responsibility, skills and pay involved with the job will affect how it is advertised. Unskilled jobs might only be advertised in local newspapers because the firm knows there is a plentiful supply of the sort of person it needs. More skilled or highly

Most vacancies for jobs are advertised in newspapers or magazines

---

Assistant Production Editor Cheltenham

An opportunity has arisen for an *Assistant Production Editor* to assist with administrative and pre-press activities within our humanities department.

You will assess and manage all stages of the editorial and production process, including control of editors, typesetters and other external suppliers in order to deliver new books and reprints within time and cost requirements.

You will be educated to degree level and will already possess high level administrative and some editorial skills. Some knowledge of production processes would be an advantage.

Night-shift Bakery Assistant
Newent

A small, family-run bakery is looking for a bakery assistant.

Applicants should be prepared to work a busy night shift. The position is concerned mainly with packaging the bread, although some baking work is likely to be involved.

No qualifications are required, but we ask that applicants are reliable. Own transport would be an advantage.

specialised jobs might be advertised in national newspapers or specialist magazines in order to attract as many people as possible. For example, *Computer Weekly* carries advertisements for jobs working with computers all over the country.

Usually the advertisement will give the name of the company, a description of the main duties of the post, information about pay, and tell the reader how to find out further details. It is usual to indicate the closing date for applications.

THE JARGON DRAGON

shortlist – list of potentially suitable applicants to be interviewed for a job

Drawing up a shortlist

Once the closing date has passed the selection process begins. The first stage of selection is to draw up a **shortlist**. At the short-listing stage the people who will be involved in the selection process examine the applications and compare them to the job specification. The purpose of shortlisting is to decide who to interview and who to reject. Some organisations will grade each application against each point in the job specification while others will give an overall grade or make a decision to interview based on the overall quality of the application in relation to the job specification. The applicants who meet the requirements of the job specification are then invited for interview.

Interviewing applicants

The interview is really just a conversation between the applicant and the firm's representatives to find out more about each other and decide if they are suitable for each other. However, it does not usually feel like this for the person being interviewed! Because interviews can be stressful it is important that both the applicant and the interviewer are well prepared if they are to find out as much as possible about each other.

Advice for applicants
- Arrive a few minutes early. Check bus and train times well in advance. If possible do the journey a few days before so you can find your way easily.
- Dress comfortably but smartly.
- Find out as much as you can about the organisation before you go for interview. This will help you understand what is

An interview allows the applicant and the company to find out more about each other

said and to ask sensible questions. Perhaps they have a website. At least look at their advertising material in order to be prepared.

- Have some questions about the job and the company in mind. This shows that you have taken the trouble to prepare for the interview.
- Try to anticipate some of the questions. This helps you prepare better answers. Avoid answering only 'yes' or 'no' – give detailed answers if possible. If you don't understand a question, say so.
- Mind your manners! Be polite, shake hands, wait to be invited to sit down and don't smoke.

Advice for interviewers

- Make sure that you have read the application forms before the interview.
- Prepare a list of questions relevant to the job that an applicant can reasonably be expected to answer.
- Put the applicant at their ease. Make sure the interview is not interrupted by other business, avoid being aggressive and encourage the applicant to answer each of your questions fully. Do not interrupt an answer.
- Make sure that the applicant doesn't avoid answering any questions.

- Take notes of the applicant's answers for later consideration.
- Allow sufficient time for the interview to find all the relevant facts, but do not keep the other applicants waiting.

Think IT THROUGH

List three questions that you might ask an employer at an interview. List three questions an employer might ask you and write down what you would say.

Selecting the most suitable candidate

As well as the interview firms will use other tests and methods of selection to judge a person's suitability for employment with them. On the day of the interview, applicants are usually shown around the building where the successful applicant will work. This provides a chance for the applicants to meet some of the people who they could be working with. This informal 'guided tour' allows firm and applicant to make judgements about each other in a way which an interview could not.

Jobs requiring particular skills might involve a test as well as the interview. Secretaries, for example, might have to type a piece of work to show how fast and accurate their typing is; would-be bus drivers might complete a maths test to demonstrate their ability to calculate fares and give the right change. Some firms use **personality assessment** for certain types of jobs. For example, organisations that sell pensions and insurance might require individuals being considered for jobs in the sales force to complete a questionnaire about their attitudes and ambitions. This test helps the firm to judge an applicant's suitability for a job involving selling.

Most application forms will ask the applicant to name at least two **referees**. They will write you a **reference**. Employers might expect to be told about your appearance, whether you are reliable, if you are a good time keeper, if you are polite and any particular skills you might have. Sometimes potential employers ask referees to write about you while other employers will list questions they would like the referee to answer. The way in

THE JARGON DRAGON

personality assessment – psychological test to assess whether a person is suitable for a particular job

referee – person who describes an applicant to a potential employer

reference – information written about a person concerning their skills and proficiency

which references are used varies from firm to firm. Some firms will use references to decide who to interview. Others will decide who to interview and then ask for the references as part of the final selection process. Yet other organisations do not check references until after they have offered someone the job. In this situation references are merely used to check that the applicant was telling the truth – if he or she lied the job offer is withdrawn. Most firms expect you to use your previous employer as a referee and will be most suspicious if you do not do so. Other referees might be a school teacher, college lecturer, vicar, priest, imman, rabbi, youth club leader, scout or guide leader, Saturday or part-time job employer. You should avoid using close relatives – potential employers are unlikely to expect them to give an unbiased reference!

Offering the job and agreeing the conditions

Once the interview and any tests have been completed the firm should be able to make a decision about who to offer the job. If none of the applicants did very well in the interview and did not meet the job specification the company might decide not to offer anyone the job and start the recruitment process again, but usually a suitable applicant will be chosen. Depending on the firm and the sort of job involved the offer may be made in a letter or telephone call some time after the interview, or on the day of the interview.

Filling a job vacancy involves several stages

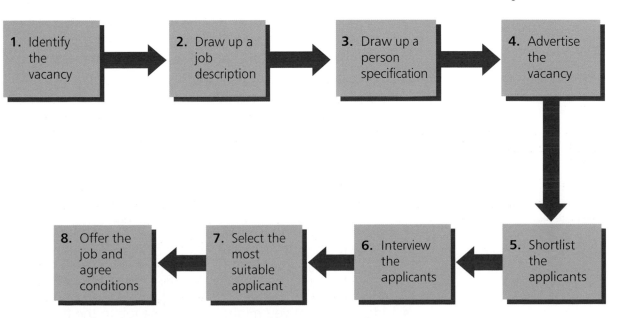

1. Identify the vacancy → 2. Draw up a job description → 3. Draw up a person specification → 4. Advertise the vacancy

8. Offer the job and agree conditions ← 7. Select the most suitable applicant ← 6. Interview the applicants ← 5. Shortlist the applicants

The person offered the job will, possibly after some negotiation about pay, accept or reject the offer. If he or she rejects the offer the next suitable applicant may be offered the job or the firm may choose to advertise again. If the applicant accepts the offer he or she will start the job at a time suitable to the firm and themselves. If the person offered the job is already in employment they will have to resign from that job and work their notice period so that the firm they are leaving can find a suitable replacement. Notice periods can be anything from a week to a month or longer, depending on the sort of job involved – teachers, for example, normally have a long notice period so that a replacement can be found and students are not left without a teacher.

At all stages of the recruitment process the business should act within the law. Particular care has to be taken not to disadvantage applicants on grounds of race, gender or disability (see pages 91–3). Both parties should act fairly. This means they should be truthful when answering questions. If you are offered the job and you accept, it is considered wrong to make applications to other firms or attend other interviews and then turn down the offer you first accepted.

Personal job applications

When inviting applications for a job a firm will say how it wants the information to be presented. Bear in mind that many other people will be after the same job, so you need to make your application stand out from the others. Your application should include the following important points:

- a description of your skills
- lists of your achievements both in and out of school – exams taken and grades, exams to be taken, club membership, etc.
- previous jobs you have had – this includes part-time jobs
- your interests, hobbies and things you do in your spare time. It's best to say more than, for example, 'reading and music' – give details
- demonstration of your enthusiasm
- ideas on what you might bring to the job in the future.

Letter of application

Sometimes you are asked to send a letter giving the necessary personal information, saying why you want the job and why you think you will be able to do it. Your letter of application should be well laid out. A letter of application lets the **applicant** present themselves in a way which suits them best and allows the employer to see how well applicants can express themselves. A disadvantage for both employer and applicant is that important details might be overlooked.

THE JARGON DRAGON

applicant – person applying for a job

Application form

An application form asks for the basic information an employer needs

An application form is a very common method of getting information about possible employees. The advantage to employers of using an application form is that it gives them all the information they need in a clear style and standard layout. Applicants can see what information the employer needs and can be sure what they say is what is needed. Wherever possible, try to type an application form or hand-write it neatly using black ink. This makes it easier for the firm to read and photocopy the form.

Some applicants think there is not enough space on the form to express themselves fully, and the restrictions on space in an application form might leave the employer short of important information. It is often acceptable to use extra sheets if necessary but these can be hard to follow unless they are clearly identified and linked to the application form.

APPLICATION FORM

PATRICK D. CALLAGHAN
WINE MERCHANT

Please complete this form in black ink or type.

Post applied for: _____

Name: _____

Address: _____

Telephone No: _____

School/College attended | Dates | Qualifications and grades

Previous employers and addresses | Start date | Leave date | Salary | Duties | Reason for leaving

Please give details of any hobbies or interests.

Please give the name and address of two referees. One should be your current or most recent employer

Please add any other points to support your application in a covering letter.

Where did you see this post advertised? _____

I declare that the information given in this application is accurate.

Signed: _____ Date: _____

Curriculum vitae

You might be asked to send a **CV**. This is short for curriculum vitae, which is a brief account of your qualifications, background and experience. You can lay these out as you think best but should contain the information mentioned on page 114. A CV allows applicants to present themselves in a way which suits them best. Copies of the same CV can be sent to more than one employer, which saves time for the applicant. Employers find that CVs give them lots of information but the different styles used by different applicants make it difficult to be sure that all the necessary information has been presented.

CURRICULUM VITAE

Name:	Jennifer White
Date of Birth:	31st October 1983
Address:	41 Gresty Crescent CREWE Cheshire CW1 1DU
Telephone:	01270 34567
School Attended:	John Partington Comprehensive Littlehampton Road CREWE CW3 5TT
Date of leaving:	June 1999
Examination Results:	GCSE Business Studies A GCSE English Language C GCSE Biology D GCSE French D
Hobbies:	Gymnastics – I represented my school for three years. Music – I sang in the school choir.
Previous Experience:	I worked as a Saturday Sales Assistant in a shoe shop for two years.
Referees	Mr H Tomlinson Headteacher John Partington Comprehensive Littlehampton Road CREWE CW3 5TT Ms J Brady Manageress Tite Fit Shoe Shop Market Street CREWE CW4 6KK

A CV gives you more control over how to present information

Record of achievement

Many school leavers have a record of achievement when they leave school. If an employer can find the time to read it the record of achievement can often be more informative than a short CV or application form. A record of achievement helps both employer and applicant by providing lots of information. However, this means they are hard to use before the applicant gets an interview. At the interview stage the applicant can use their record of achievement to provide good evidence of their successes and interests.

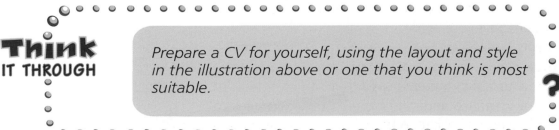

Think IT THROUGH

Prepare a CV for yourself, using the layout and style in the illustration above or one that you think is most suitable.

Staff development and training

For a firm to be able to develop goods and services that meet its customers' needs it is important that the employees are kept up to date with changes and developments which affect their jobs and careers. This benefits not only the firm but also the employees. The Personnel Department is normally involved in the process of staff development. When you start a new job you will be shown where things are kept and how activities are organised, and usually given more details about what the firm does and how it has developed. You will be given details of health and safety rules as they apply to the firm. This training at the start of the job is called induction training. Once you start the job you should expect to receive ongoing training, which can be of two basic types.

induction training – training given at the start of a new job to show how the activities of the firm are organised

ongoing training – training to develop new skills, given either at work or outside

On-the-job training

This is where the employee learns new skills while at work. Usually this sort of training will involve the trainee – learner – watching someone carrying out the work they have to learn and then copying them. This sort of training provides the chance to discuss work with other employees. On-the-job training has the advantage of being cheaper to provide than other sorts of training as production is not disrupted as it would be if the employee went outside the firm to learn new skills. A disadvantage of on the job training is that the product being produced by the trainee might, at least at first, be sub-standard or result in high amounts of wastage. On-the-job trainers might not be particularly skilled unless they have been taught how to teach others.

Off-the-job training

Employees develop new skills by being taken out of work, perhaps to a college or the firm's training centre. Off-the-job training allows the trainee to develop skills and knowledge without the distractions of work and is usually carried out with specialist staff who can provide more detailed knowledge about the work being done. This sort of training can be expensive as specialist staff wages have to be paid and production is lost as the employee is away from work. Off-the-job training is commonly organised on a day release basis or a block release basis. Day-release trainees are released from work one day a week for their training while block release trainees might be trained for days or weeks at a time before going back to work. Some employees have off-the-job training through going to night classes at colleges in the area where they live.

A firm's decision of style of training will be affected by details such as cost, the type of work involved, the sort of skills which have to be learned and other practical details. In all cases the decision will be guided by the contribution training makes to improving the firm's future prospects.

Most young or junior staff will be expected to undergo some sort of training when they start work. Many school leavers are trained through the Modern Apprenticeship Scheme, in which the government supports employers who provide training that helps young people get NVQ or other vocational qualifications. Older people will have access to government schemes such as New Deal to prepare them to enter work with the necessary skills.

Appraisal or performance reviews

Training is not the only way of improving the work performance of an organisation's staff. Some organisations use a system of appraisal, or performance review. In this review an employee's standards of work are discussed and assessed by the employee and his or her manager. The aim of appraisal is to help the workers be better at their jobs, to the benefit of both firm and worker. Different methods of appraisal are used but they have several features in common.

- Appraisal involves an employee discussing their work with their manager.
- The employee might fill in a questionnaire before the appraisal interview, which becomes the starting point of the discussion.
- Points dealt with in any appraisal system might include how well the employee works with others, what they think their strengths and weaknesses are, what their career ambitions are and any ideas they have for improving the way their part of the firm works.
- It is usual for the manager to write a report of the discussion – sometimes in agreement with the employee – and the report is placed on the employee's file and used to start the discussion at the next appraisal interview.

case study

Ambition

The government has announced the launch of *Ambition:IT*, a £50 million partnership with businesses in the information and communications technology sector to help 5,000 unemployed people into employment, and improve the IT skills of 15,000 more. The government estimates that by 2006 90% of all jobs will require basic keyboard and ICT competence, compared with 70% today. Ambition will have three elements:

- Ambition challenge – projects using IT to improve *New Deal* delivery.

- First ambition – helping disadvantaged people train for the European Computer Driving Licence (a computing qualification).

- Career ambition – a three-year pilot programme, running in five areas with high IT demand and concentrations of lone parents and unemployed people. London, Manchester, Birmingham, Leeds, South Yorkshire, Liverpool, Tyneside, Glasgow and Edinburgh have been shortlisted. The sponsor firms are FI Group, Microsoft, Cisco, Sage, BT, Cap Gemini, Siemens, Post Office, IBM and EDS. Later the Government 'hope to work with groups of SMEs (Small and Medium Enterprises) so that they can also take advantage of career ambition.'

Based on a briefing on the TUC website http://www.tuc.org.uk/ **October 2001.**

Q1 *Why is the government prepared to invest in training unemployed people in new technology?*

Q2 *What advantages will the scheme bring to the SMEs mentioned in the briefing?*

- The appraisal report will usually summarise the discussion between the manager and the employee and will list any goals that were agreed (e.g. the employee might agree to try to improve their timekeeping and/or the manager might agree to find them a place on a training course).

- In some organisations the appraisal report will be taken into account when considering employees for promotion or salary increases.

Appraisal interviews

Appraisal interviews usually take place annually but a good manager will regularly review the work of his or her staff in order to anticipate any problems. The advantage of appraisal interviewing is that it allows mangers and employees to discuss, in a constructive way, any problems the employee might be having and encourages the employee to put forward their ideas and suggestions. Such discussions can create a good working atmosphere, and help the organisation to work as well as possible. A disadvantage of appraisal interviews is that they are time consuming – usually lasting at least half an hour – and take the manager and employee away from other work.

THE JARGON DRAGON

job rotation – workers regularly swap jobs with other people in their section

Retraining in new technology or new working practices

Retraining is now a common feature of modern business. This retraining can be done on the job, block or day release (see page 117), or it can be done by **job rotation**. Job rotation can prevent boredom and helps the employee to understand how other parts of the organisation work and make them familiar with the technology and processes used elsewhere in the business. This makes them feel more involved with the firm as they can understand how their work 'fits in' with what other people do. It leads to a more flexible workforce as individuals are capable of doing several different jobs and develops team working. Being able to do several jobs means that the employee has a wider range of skills to offer if they decide to seek promotion or work for a different firm.

Think IT THROUGH

What are the advantages and disadvantages of introducing new technology at work from the point of view of (a) the employer; (b) the employee?

National awards

National awards such as Investors in People (an on-going standard of quality for staff development and training) and National Training Awards (an annual competition for exceptionally effective training) are given by government representatives to businesses who demonstrate to independent assessors that they invest in the training needs of their employees. You might want to check if a prospective employer has these awards as they show a commitment to your future training and career development. Firms who have these awards are allowed to display their logos on advertisements and letterheads.

INVESTORS IN PEOPLE

Firms with this award have shown commitment to the development of their employees (produced by permission of Investors in People UK®)

Customer service – why customers are important

Customer service is important in helping business win and keep customers. Once they identify customer needs businesses can make the best use of employees and technology to meet these needs.

Good customers who make regular purchases provide a steady stream of income for the business and supply information, through their buying habits, about how well the company's products are selling. Repeat business is an important factor in business success.

If the business gets its customer service right it will be able to:

- gain and retain customers
- increase customer satisfaction and loyalty
- improve the image and reputation of the business
- provide information about how the product is used
- keep or increase its **market share**
- increase **sales revenue** and profits.

THE JARGON DRAGON

market share – the percentage of possible customers who buy one particular firm's product

sales revenue – money a firm receives from selling things

Customers and their expectations

Internal customers

These are people who work in other parts of the business and rely on their colleagues to supply goods or services. For instance, a manager at Comet who asks for a report about this week's sales of DVDs is the internal customer of the person who has to write the report.

External customers

Individuals or firms who make purchases from outside the business are external customers. If you buy a DVD from Comet, you are their external customer.

Customer expectations

The successful business is one that meets customer expectations.

Good value products

Regardless of whether the product is a packet of sweets or a CD player, its price must be what the customer is willing and able to pay. The product should be capable of being easily used and understood – in other words it must be practical. Most of all the product must be reliable and do what the sellers claim it is capable of doing.

Rapid response to enquiries

Customers will expect to have their enquiries dealt with promptly and knowledgeably. Slow response to letters, unanswered telephones and long queues to find information are all off-putting and can result in lost sales.

Clear and honest information

Customers will ask for information before they make a purchase. This will help them to compare rival products. The price of the item is an important piece of information. Customers often ask questions about the performance of an item (e.g. 'How many miles per gallon will this car do?', 'Are these boots waterproof?').

They also request information about environmental or 'green' concerns, e.g. 'Does the product have side effects which damage the environment?' 'Was it tested on animals?' Questions about when an item can be delivered are also common and sometimes fast delivery can help take a sale away from a rival.

Some customers have concerns about the way products are developed and businesses should be aware of these

Information about suitable products

When buying something for the first time customers will ask for guidance from sales staff, who they expect to know something about the items for sale and the alternatives available. This need for advice is most common with expensive or complicated items such as cars, video players and computers. If the sales assistant can make helpful comments which simplify the situation this will help the customer make a decision to buy. When offering advice the sales assistant should be able to show the customer how far the items on sale meet their needs. A customer who feels they have received honest and helpful information is more likely to be satisfied and recommend you to friends or buy from you again.

Help with individual or general issues

A customer will eventually find out if you have mislead them. If you have exaggerated the benefits of the product or sold something which you know will be unsuitable, or is more expensive than they need, the customer will be dissatisfied and reduce your chances of a repeat sale in the future. They will tell their friends and relatives how they feel. If you match your sale to the customer's needs and the amount they can afford they are more likely to come back again and praise you to others. This is known as 'word of mouth' advertising, and is very effective in getting new customers.

Care and attention

A customer who feels well treated is more likely to come back. A customer who feels poorly treated will not make a purchase and is likely to tell everyone he or she knows about the way you have treated them. This may put people off buying your goods or services in the future. Remember to be polite, listen to the customer and stop your personal feeling getting in the way of making the customer feel satisfied.

After-sales service

How well a customer is treated after they have bought an item is almost as important as how well they are treated before they make the purchase. Expensive or complicated items are more likely to be offered an after sales service. Examples of good after-sales service include:

- being able to phone your computer supplier to ask for advice with a computer problem
- low cost or free servicing of a new car
- receiving a phone call from the supplier to check that the product is satisfactory
- being offered discount on related items (e.g. reduced price on video tapes bought with a video recorder).

Customer satisfaction

Businesses need to measure customer satisfaction in order to find out what improvements should be made to the goods or services they offer. They use a number of methods to do this.

Analysing sales performance

Sales can be analysed by looking at the value of sales, the number of customers and details of purchases through loyalty card schemes. These are the schemes that give points when purchases are made. The number of points is related to the value of the purchases made.

Recording the number of complaints or returned goods

High levels of complaints or many returned goods can indicate faults in the production process that should be looked at.

Making comparisons with competitors

By comparing its performance with competitors in the same line of business a firm can make judgements about its level of performance in relation to customer opinion.

Research

Businesses will carry out market research into customer opinions about its own goods and services and those of its rivals. Large firms will employ the services of a market research agency such as MORI or may have a dedicated marketing department to undertake such work. It is important that any market research is done using people who are representative of the potential users of the product. It would be better, for example, to interview teenagers about new developments in skateboard design than people in their 70s. Several different methods of research can be used.

On-the-spot questions from staff

This common method involves the researcher stopping people in the street or interviewing them over the telephone.

Observation

This may be used to research the sales of a new product. People will be invited to try the new product and researchers will observe their use of the product. From their observations researchers may suggest changes in design or in how instructions are written to improve the use of the product.

Questionnaires

People may be brought to an office or hotel to complete a questionnaire under supervision of the people doing the research. Sometimes they are completed at home and returned by post. Care must be taken to make sure the questionnaire is clear.

Customer panels of interviewers

Customer panels involve members of the public trying the product and then discussing it with interviewers. If it is a new frozen food item, for example, questions may be asked about taste, texture and appearance of the product. Sometimes different versions of the product will be compared by the panel.

Website

Most large businesses and many smaller firms have their own website. These have facilities for customers to respond directly to what they see on the website.

Businesses need to do all they can to find out the opinions of their customers

E-mails

E-mails can be used in the same way as postal surveys. The advantage is that they take less time to communicate the information.

Investigating customer service

Customer service depends on a number of important features. These vary from business to business.

Products

As we have seen, the right quality at the right price is very important.

Packaging

Good packaging will show the product to best advantage. Well designed packaging will create the impression that there is more in the packet than there is. It will also help in the way the item is displayed in the shop, for instance if it is easy to stack. Good packaging will also keep the product safe from damage.

Safety

Safety is an important consideration. When a product is sold the person making the sale should ensure there are no risks of injury to the user. A child's toys should have no sharp edges or loose parts that a young child could swallow. Electrical goods should be checked for safety, as should any sorts of tools or equipment.

Information

Clear information about the product and how to use it is essential. As well as traditional advertising more and more firms will display information about their products on their websites.

Staff

When you deal with a customer you have the chance to either put them off your business for ever or to make them so happy with your firm that they come back again. If they don't come back to make further purchases the profits of the firm will suffer. How can you make sure customers return?

- **Be friendly** – greet the customer, by name if possible, either on the telephone or in person. But don't be *too* friendly and do not use first names unless invited to do so.
- **Look smart** – well presented staff make a good impression and make customers more confident in the business.
- **Listen** to what the customer wants – do not interrupt but ask questions to check that you understand after they have finished speaking.
- **Be polite** – this is very difficult with some customers, but remember your job might depend on how well you deal with awkward customers. The look on your face and how you stand show what you are thinking so remember to *look* polite as well as *being* polite.
- **Keep your promises** – in all your dealings with customers make sure that you can do what you promise to do. For example, do not promise to make a delivery on Thursday just to get rid of the customer if you know a delivery on that day is not possible. If you promise to make a phone call or send a letter – do it! Research has shown that customers talk to more friends and relatives about a bad experience with a firm that they do about a good experience. If you let a customer down word gets round fast. This will deter customers from even approaching your business to see if you can help them. This will of course lead to reduced sales and profits.

Premises

Clean and well lit premises make a good impression. Larger premises should be well signposted so customers can navigate their way around. It is important that disabled people can access all parts of the premises. Features such as car parking, toilets, cafe and children's play area are not only appreciated by customers but make it more likely they will come and stay longer.

Pleasant premises make a good impression on visitors

Delivery

This is particularly important with large or bulky items such as cookers, televisions, refrigerators or beds – although grocers, butchers and newsagents sometimes offer a delivery service for small items to make shopping more convenient for their customers. Supermarkets such as Tesco and Sainsbury provide Internet shopping facilities and will deliver the selected goods to the customer. Sometimes a delivery service is free or at a low cost to encourage customers to make a purchase. The most expensive part of a delivery service is the wages of the delivery staff, and so some shops lend or hire roof racks or vans to customers so that they can take their purchases home. Businesses buying large quantities from other businesses find transport costs are expensive and will be attracted to suppliers who are able to offer a free or low cost delivery service. Speed and reliability are key features of a delivery service.

After-sales care

How a business deals with its customers after the sale has been made is important. Dealing swiftly and fairly with any complaints can make a good impression on the customer. Honouring guarantees and providing repairs or replacements can also make a good impression. A number of firms now offer a 'no-quibble' guarantee to exchange goods or refund payments without question if the customer is dissatisfied. This encourages the customer to make a purchase and increases sales.

Other features

Offering customer care phone lines or Internet information can help make customers feel appreciated and deal with their enquiries about the products they have purchased or are considering. Being able to buy more expensive items on credit, or to defer payments for a period, helps the customer make the purchase they want. Some goods are sold on credit without the need for a deposit. Staff training in customer service can help improve the service. It is possible to obtain an NVQ in Customer Service.

Think IT THROUGH

Look at advertisements in this week's local newspaper. List the ways, with examples, of how businesses are trying to offer customer service.

?

Protecting the customer

The customer is protected by various laws and regulations which businesses need to observe.

Health and safety

The customer must be made fully aware of all the safety features of the product. Where products meet the standards of independent, respected organisations, this should be pointed out. The British Standards Institution (BSI) lays down standards for certain products and services. These standards represent an accepted level of quality and safety. If a product is produced to these standards it will carry the BSI symbol – the kitemark. Customers find this reassuring.

There are other safety symbols and schemes to consider. For instance, the Corgi scheme represents a minimum satisfactory standard which gas appliance fitters meet. Gas fitters cannot get Corgi approval unless they meet minimum safety standards and have passed the relevant tests. Electrical goods that meet the British Elecrotechnical Approvals Board (BEAB) standard will carry their mark, which shows that the product is safe to use.

Sale of products

It is illegal to sell goods that are not fit for the purpose for which they were sold. This means that goods that are advertised with particular claims should meet these claims – e.g. hiking boots should stand up to hard wear and tear. The law requires that goods are of **merchantable quality**. For example, a new car could not be legally sold with several defects or scratches.

merchantable quality – goods must be of the standard expected of similar goods purchased in the same way

Labelling of products

The goods must meet the description of them, even if the description was a verbal one. It is illegal to make a false description of the goods. A table made of pine cannot be advertised as being made out of oak, for example. Prices must also be accurately advertised. An item cannot be advertised as being at a reduced price unless it has been on sale at the higher price for 28 consecutive days in the previous six months. If it has not been on sale at the higher price for the 28 day period the seller must indicate this – for example by labelling it 'Yesterday's price £3.00, Today's price £1.99'.

Misuse of information

The Data Protection Act protects customers as well as employees. The law allows customers to see data about themselves held by businesses. Companies can only use data about customers for the purpose for which it was collected and they must ask permission to use the data for other purposes.

case study

Millions unaware of basic rights

Millions of people do not know the full extent of their employment, benefits and consumer rights according to a new National Association of Citizens Advice Bureaux (NACAB) survey carried out in 2001.

NACAB asked 2010 people a series of six questions concerning their basic rights and more than 56% of those replying got more than three of the answers wrong. Only *one* person got all the answers right. People in London were most likely to get more than three wrong.

NACAB chief executive David Harker said: 'This survey shows that, understandably, people don't immediately have all the necessary information to hand and explains why sources of information and advice such as the Citizens Advice Bureau are so essential.'

Main findings from the survey show that:

- *42% of people believed the national minimum wage to be higher than it actually is.*

- *57% were unaware that people in full-time employment are entitled to four weeks paid annual holiday.*

- *More than half – 51% of people – were unaware that they are entitled to a full refund when reconditioned second-hand goods turn out to be faulty.*

Information on the subjects covered in the survey and in general can be obtained via a local CAB. Many bureaux throughout the country now deliver advice in places like health centres, hospitals, courts and prisons, libraries and community centres or by accessing Adviceguide, at www.adviceguide.org.uk.

Based on NACAB press release September 2001.

Q1 *What were the main findings of the survey?*

Q2 *Name three ways to find information mentioned in the article.*

The Consumers' Association has published a series of 24 leaflets explaining people's legal rights on everything from welfare benefits and employment to problems with goods and services. These can be obtained from local bureaux, libraries and community centres or by calling the Legal Services Commission leaflet line on 0845 3000 343. Each local authority will have a trading standards department, the next port of call after the CAB concerning consumer rights. Their number can be found in the local telephone directory.

Find the address of your local Citizens' Advice Bureau in the telephone book, Yellow Pages or on the Internet (www.nacab.org.uk). Find out about the help and advice they can provide to customers who feel unfairly treated in relation to products they have purchased. Present this as a wall display.

FIND IT OUT

What's in this unit?

This unit will show you the importance of information technology in all aspects of business activities, particularly in tracking the flow of money in and out of a business. Spreadsheets are used to record financial activities and help make plans.

In this unit you will learn of some of the financial planning and recording systems used in business, and how to interpret the information that certain business documents provide. The unit also discusses the role of IT in helping to reduce costs and make business more effective and efficient.

Business Finance 3

In this unit you will learn about:

Financial documents used to make a business purchase

THE JARGON DRAGON

transaction – the act of buying or selling

Cadbury Schweppes sells its products in over 400 countries. Coca Cola has over 16 million customers. Tesco has over 650 stores. Large businesses like these rely on well organised systems to track what is being bought and sold and to record the flow of money into and out of the business.

The sales **transactions** of businesses need to be accurately recorded. The financial documents used are important in recording each step of the process. Accurate financial documents help businesses to:

- track transactions
- avoid paying too much or not enough
- avoid wasting time in having to correct errors
- plan income and expenditure
- make sure that records for tax purposes are accurate
- make sure customers are not inconvenienced by incorrect or late deliveries
- make sure customers are not inconvenienced by payment requests for the wrong amount.

The presentation of these documents will vary from business to business. This section helps you understand what should be contained in each of the main business documents.

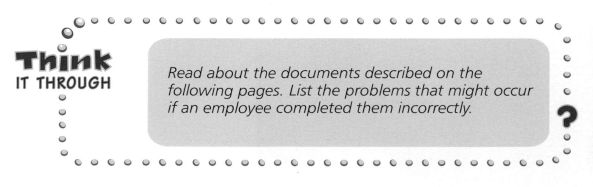

Think IT THROUGH

Read about the documents described on the following pages. List the problems that might occur if an employee completed them incorrectly.

Purchase order

When a firm wishes to make a purchase it will send out a purchase order to its supplier. Normally it will have considered the prices of goods and services provided by several firms before sending, or *placing* the order. The order will have the firm's name, address, phone number and other contact details. Each order is separately numbered so it can be easily identified. Some firms use computerised stock control systems to automatically send orders when their records show that stocks are low. This allows clerical staff to work on other tasks.

Delivery note

The delivery note is sent along with the goods to the purchaser. It includes details such as quantity, type and size of goods being delivered as well as the usual contact information. If someone in the receiving organisation signs the document, the delivery note can also be used as proof of delivery. When orders are sent in more than one delivery the delivery note is a useful way of tracking how much more is to come.

Goods received note

This document will be signed by someone from the firm receiving the goods. Its purpose is to show that the goods have been received. Often a signed copy of the delivery note will be used as the goods received note.

INVOICE

Brookside Plc ①

Mosstown

Manchester M1 9GJ

Telephone 0161 689 1234

Fax: 0161 689 5678

Date	1 March 2002 ⑤	INVOICE NUMBER K82/498 ③	
To:	Castle Cary Plc ②	YOUR ORDER NO.: 39876 ④	
	5 Barlow Street		
	Hanley's Ford		
	HA5 2RD		

Quantity	Description	Unit Price	Total Price
50 ⑦	Packs of three C90 audio tapes ⑥	£10.00 ⑧	£500.00 ⑨
25	Pack of ten notebooks	£10.00	£250.00
	GOOD TOTAL		£750.00 ⑩
	Plus VAT @ 17.5		£131.25 ⑪
	INVOICE TOTAL		£881.25
	E & OE ⑬		
	Terms of payment:		
	2.5% one month		
	5% 7 days ⑫		

The invoice should be carefully checked against the goods received and the goods ordered notes

Invoice

An invoice is normally sent when goods have been delivered to a firm or some sort of service has been provided. It is often sent in advance, to warn the customer that the goods are on the way. The invoice shows what has been supplied and how much money is owed. The information about what has been supplied should be checked against the goods received or the service provided to ensure that they match, otherwise you could be paying for something you had not received. You should also check that the invoice details are the same as those on the order form to check you have got what you asked for. Many firms have computerised their systems for dealing with customers' accounts and invoices are often produced by computer. The style of invoices vary from firm to firm, but you can expect them to have the following information:

1 Name, address, telephone and fax number of supplier
2 Name and address of customer
3 Invoice number
4 Order number
5 Date invoice issued
6 Name/description of items purchased
7 Number of items purchased
8 Price of each item
9 Total price of each item
10 Total price of all items on the invoice
11 Amount of VAT to be paid
12 Details of discounts – prompt payment can lead to reduced prices. In this example the cost will be reduced by 5% if payment is received within seven days of receiving the invoice
13 E and O E – this stands for Error and Omissions Excepted. This is a statement that allows the supplier to ask for further payment if they have made a mistake (error) or missed anything out (omission) on the invoice.

Most firms do not usually pay the invoice immediately but wait until the end of the month or until they receive a statement from their supplier (see page 141). The invoice is a very useful document for checking that the goods received were the ones requested on the order.

Credit note

Sometimes customers don't find out mistakes in delivery until after they have paid for the goods or services on a particular invoice. For example, your business might have paid for a 100 metre roll of fencing wire but found out it was only a 10 metre roll when you came to use it. Such a problem should be explained to, and a solution agreed with, the supplier, who may wish to check the situation before sending you a credit note for the amount you have been overcharged. The credit note shows that the supplier owes you that amount of money. You can present the credit note when you make your next payment to that firm to reduce the amount you have to pay (see below).

The style of credit notes will vary, depending on the business issuing them. Many firms have computerised their systems for dealing with customers' accounts and this document will often be produced by computer. Some firms print them in red so they stand out from other documents. When a computerised system creates a credit note it will automatically update the customer's payment details to show the change caused by the credit note. You can expect to find the following information on a credit note:

A credit note will be issued if the customer has paid too much for some reason

---

CREDIT NOTE

Telephone 0161 699 1234
Fax 0161 689 5678

Brookside Plc ①
Mosstown
Manchester M1 9GJ

To: Castle Cary Plc ②
      5 Barlow Street
      Hanley's Ford HA5 2RD

Credit Note   CN82/498 ③
Invoice Number K82/498 ④
Date   8 March 2002 ⑤

Quantity	Description	UNit Price	Total Price
3 ⑦	Packs of three C90 audio tapes ⑥	£10.00 ⑧	£30.00 ⑨
	Packing damaged and returned VAT @ 17.5%		£5.25 ⑪
	TOTAL PRICE E & OE ⑫ Carriage paid		£35.25 ⑩

1. Name, address, telephone and fax number of supplier
2. Name and address of customer
3. Credit note number
4. Number of invoice causing credit note to be issued
5. Date credit note issued
6. Name/description of items faulty/returned/damaged, etc.
7. Number of items faulty/returned/damaged, etc.
8. Price of each item
9. Total price of each item
10. Total price of all items on the invoice
11. Amount of VAT to be refunded
12. E and O E – this stands for Error and Omissions Excepted. This statement allows the supplier to ask for further payment if they have made a mistake (error) or missed anything out (omission) on the credit note.

> *Who benefits most from issuing a credit note?*

? Think IT THROUGH

Statement of account

When goods are bought on **credit** using orders and invoices, etc. the customer will have an account with the supplier. They will regularly receive statements from the supplier showing the state of the account – how much money is owed and the business transactions that have taken place since the last statement of account was sent. The statement won't show details of every item bought, only the value of each payment, credit note and invoice since the last statement.

THE JARGON DRAGON

credit – providing a product or service to a customer and being paid sometime afterwards

The value of any credit notes and payments received will be taken away from the value of the invoices. Statements of account are normally sent monthly. Many firms produce their statements automatically by computer. The computerised system avoids the needs for office staff to do many time-consuming calculations. The appearance of statements of account will vary from firm to firm but each should contain the following information:

1 Name, address and telephone and fax number of supplier
2 Name and address of customer
3 Account number
4 Statement number
5 Date statement issued
6 Date of each invoice or credit note issued
7 Description of documents
8 Value of debits – amounts owed by the customer
9 Value of credits – amounts received by or owed to the supplier
10 The balance – the difference between the figures in 8 and 9. This is the amount to be paid
11 Amount of VAT to be paid
12 E and O E – This stands for Error and Omissions Excepted. This is a statement which allows the supplier to ask for further payment if they have made a mistake (error) or missed anything out (omission) on the invoice

The statement is a summary of what business transactions have taken place – it shows how much is owed and is a request for payment

STATEMENT				
Telephone 0161 699 1234 Fax 0161 689 5678			Brookside Plc ① Mosstown Manchester M1 9GJ	
To: Castle Cary Plc ② 5 Barlow Street Hanley's Ford HA5 2RD			Account number 12323 ③ Statement Number 513 ④ Date 8 March 2002 ⑤	
Date	Goods	Debt	Credit	Balance
1988 ⑥ 1 March	Goods supplied on invoice no K82/498 ⑦	£881.25 ⑧		£881.25
6 March	Returns 3 items Credit Note CN82/498		£30.00 ⑨	£851.25 ⑩
	VAT @ 17.5%		£5.25	£846.00 ⑪
	E & OE ⑫			

THE JARGON DRAGON

remittance – payment and details

Remittance advice slip

Firms will often request payment for goods or services be made directly into their bank account. The **remittance** advice slip will be sent by the purchaser to tell the seller that they have made a payment into the purchaser's bank account and what this payment is for. The purchaser can then use this information to check that the details are correct when looking at their own financial records.

Cheques

A cheque is a written instruction from an account holder to their bank to pay the person named on the cheque a certain amount of money. Cheques are more secure to use than cash because they can only be used after the person who owns the bank account has signed them. Using cheques reduces the risks of carrying or storing money, because criminals cannot use stolen cheques as easily as cash.

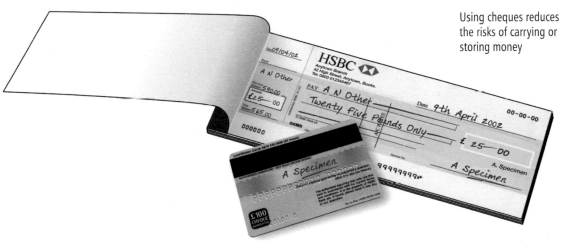

Using cheques reduces the risks of carrying or storing money

Most firms will only accept cheques from individuals if the person paying has a cheque guarantee card from their bank with the signature of the person paying. The cheque guarantee card promises that the bank will pay for the purchase, up to the value of £100 or £50 (depending on the type of card used), even if the person has no money in their bank account. If larger amounts are involved advance agreement from the bank will be necessary. The selling firm may check with the buyer's bank that he or she has sufficient funds to meet the debt. This is called a credit check. When one business pays another by cheque a guarantee card is not usually required, but the selling firm will normally carry out a **credit check** on the buying firm before doing business with them.

THE JARGON DRAGON

credit check – when a seller makes sure that a purchaser is able to pay for items purchased

A cheque can be used to show that payment has been made and received. There is space – called a stub – on each page of a cheque book for the owner to write down what has been paid out. If a person does not have enough money in their account to pay the amount on the cheque the bank may refuse to pay up. This is called 'bouncing' a cheque. The bank will charge the person writing the cheque a fee for each cheque that bounces. A bank statement will show which cheques have been paid out. Cheques have to be written out and this can make the business transaction rather slow. To overcome this, firms that send out lots of cheque payments will print them by computer.

Computers can save time in processing cheque payments

Receipts

When the seller has received the customer's payment they may send a receipt to confirm that the payment has been received. The buyer then has evidence for future use if there is a dispute about payment. Because cheque payments are recorded in the details of each firm's bank account receipts are not normally used for cheques, or for direct payments to the seller's account. They will most often be used when cash is the method of payment.

FIND IT OUT

Use the methods of purchases below as headings. List underneath each heading how customers would pay for the items listed and what documents would be used. Shop – jacket, Mail order – CD, Internet – book, Shop – furniture, Market stall – sweets, Garage – second-hand car.

Computer-based systems

Computers can make dealing with financial documents a lot easier. Computer systems can find information very quickly and take up less space than paper systems. Certain systems let several people have access to the same record at the same time, so that records can be kept up to date very easily. For example, warehouse staff can use the computer to see what orders have been placed and sent out, and decide whether or not they need to prepare space to receive a delivery. With a well run computer-based system linked records (such as all the invoices sent to one customer between particular dates) can be found very easily. Once the computer system has been correctly installed it is generally very reliable.

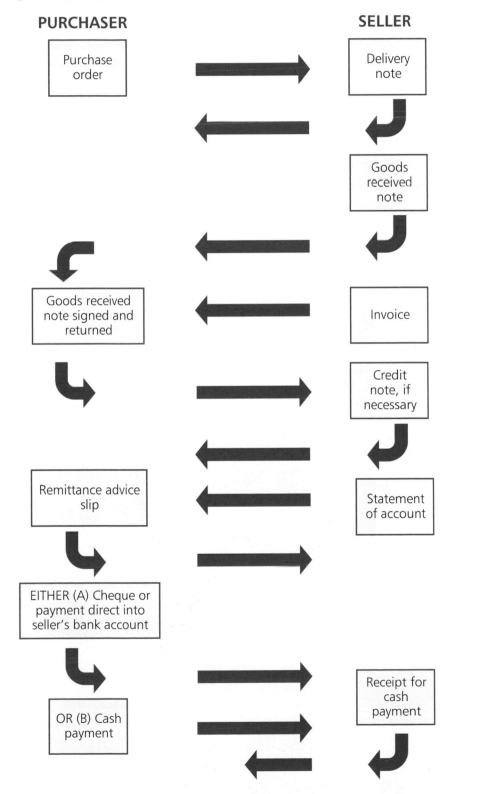

PURCHASER

SELLER

Purchase order

Delivery note

Goods received note

Goods received note signed and returned

Invoice

Credit note, if necessary

Remittance advice slip

Statement of account

EITHER (A) Cheque or payment direct into seller's bank account

OR (B) Cash payment

Receipt for cash payment

The flow of documents between buyer and seller

As well as holding the financial records on the computer system, duplicate or back-up copies of information should be made on each day and kept in a different room from the computer, ideally in a waterproof and fireproof secure cabinet.

Disadvantages of computer-based systems

- Computer-based systems are expensive to set up, because of the cost of the computers and other equipment such as printers that are needed.
- Linking computers together in a network – which is a very efficient way of organising them – can also be costly.
- Sensitive electronic equipment like computers can be easily damaged by moisture or vibration.
- Training staff to use computer systems can be time consuming and more expensive than training them to use traditional paper-based methods.

Staff need training when new computer systems are introduced

Think
IT THROUGH

Many people worry about unemployment and about high prices. Is it unfair on the general public for businesses to use computers and other technology to reduce their workforce and costs?

Methods of making and receiving payments

There are several ways of making and receiving payments. Many businesses have to convert currency from customers overseas into their own currency, something that computers can do automatically. The **Euro** has removed the problem of currency conversion for the countries of the European Union that have adopted it. Several payment methods are available, regardless of what currency is being used.

THE JARGON DRAGON

Euro – currency shared by several countries in the European Union, represented by the symbol €

Cash

Cash is the most commonly used method of payment – notes and coins are a quick and convenient way of paying for items. Cash is accepted by anyone and using it is a very straightforward way of paying for something. Once the money is handed over and the goods or services received the business transaction is completed. However, because it is so widely accepted and easy to use stealing cash is a popular activity with criminals! There is no way of proving who owns particular coins or notes. For this reason businesses which deal with a lot of cash need very good security systems. Individuals should not carry more cash than they need at any one time. Cash is generally used in transactions involving fairly small amounts of money.

Use of the Euro has removed the problem of currency conversion for those countries that have adopted it

Cheques

If you have a current account with a bank you will probably have a cheque book containing a number of cheques that you can use to pay for goods or services. A cheque is a pre-printed letter from you to your bank asking them to give the person you name on the cheque the amount of money you ask them to. Cheques are more secure to use than cash because they can only be used after the person who has the bank account where the money is to come from has signed them. Businesses as well as individuals make use of cheques to pay for goods and services. There are more details on cheques on page 143.

Credit card

Credit cards are a popular method of payment. Visa and MasterCard are the main credit cards, although they are issued by banks and building societies under different names (e.g. Barclay Card).

All credit card holders have a personal credit limit, which tells them how much they are allowed to owe at any one time. The credit limit will vary according to a person's earnings and background. They can use their credit card to buy items up to their credit limit and then pay the amount owing either all at once or in monthly instalments. These monthly instalments must cover at least a fixed percentage of the total amount owed. The buyer also has to pay extra to the credit card company for the advantages of being able to make purchases without cash. This extra charge is known as <u>interest</u>, the price paid for borrowing money.

interest – charge for borrowing money

There is a wide range of credit and debit cards available

Credit cards are very convenient to use and buyers are attracted to businesses that accept them because they can buy things without having to pay straight away. Both buyer and seller benefit in these ways. A disadvantage for the business is that the credit card company takes a percentage of the value of the sales made using the credit card. Credit card payments can be processed manually or by computer. When payments are processed manually the seller places the card into an imprinter machine, transferring the credit card details onto a payment slip which the customer signs. The seller might make a telephone call to the card issuer to confirm that the payment does not exceed the customer's credit limit. This method means that payment may not be received by the seller until several days later. Computer-based methods mean payment is received by the seller almost immediately.

Debit cards

Switch and Delta are the two main debit cards in use. Debit cards are dealt with in the same way as credit cards but can only be used if the card holder has enough money in their account to cover the cost of purchases. The debit card does not allow the card holder to buy goods on credit – which is the purpose of a credit card.

The debit card has the convenience of the credit card without the disadvantage of having to make interest payments. From the buyer's point of view it is cheaper to use. Sellers may have to make a payment to the Debit Card organisation for using their system.

EFTPOS

Both credit cards and debit cards make use of Electronic Funds Transfer at Point of Sale (EFTPOS). When making a purchase the customer presents their debit or credit card to the sales assistant, who passes it through an electronic reader. This reads the information about the card holder's account that is stored on a special strip on the card. It then sends a message to a computer containing details of the card holder's account This computer transfers the value of the purchase to the seller's account. The till prints a slip of paper which the cardholder must sign to show they have agreed to the transaction. He or she keeps a copy of the slip, as does the seller.

EFTPOS is faster than using cheques, payment is guaranteed and the seller does not have to wait as long for payment as with cheques. It is now common for banks to issue one card that can do the job of cheque guarantee card, debit card and credit card.

Credit and debit cards are quick and convenient methods of payment and avoid the need to carry cash, although they can cost money to use

Credit transfer

Payment into a bank or building society account can be made by completing a credit transfer. A paying-in slip is completed with the details of the amount being paid and the account the money is to go to. This is a useful way of dealing with large amounts of money as it ensures funds go into the intended account in a secure way. Credit transfer could be used by one firm to pay a debt to another business.

To make a credit transfer you need to know the account number and branch details of the account you are paying into. While this system is more secure than cash it has the disadvantage of needing four or five days for the funds to move into the intended account. Sometimes there is a charge for the service if payment is not made through your own bank.

To make payment manually you can use paying-in slips available at the bank counter. Alternatively, payments can be processed by computer at the bank, with the customer needing only to check the details and sign the paying-in slip.

Direct debit

Where firms or individuals make regular transactions with another organisation direct debit can be a cheap and convenient method of payment. It is useful if the exact amount to be paid is not known in advance (e.g. gas or electricity bill). The buyer completes a form that gives the seller permission to remove from its bank account the amount they owe at a certain time each month. Once agreement has been reached, this method is carried out by computers. It is free for buyers and cheaper for sellers than carrying out the tasks manually. The system ensures payment is made on an agreed date, which helps both buyer and seller to plan their financial arrangements. Some sellers will give discounts to buyers who agree to pay by this method.

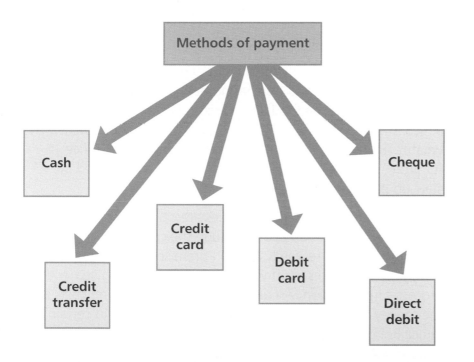

Businesses need to deal with many methods of payment

Working in pairs, prepare a wall display using leaflets and information from local banks about the advantages of using debit and credit cards. In your own words explain how credit transfers and direct debits are organised and provide completed examples of the documents used.

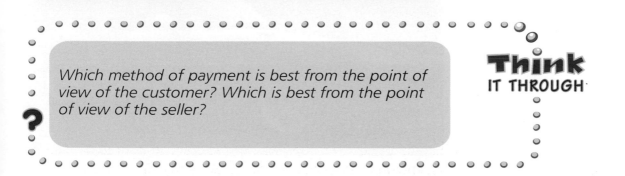

FIND IT OUT

Which method of payment is best from the point of view of the customer? Which is best from the point of view of the seller?

Think IT THROUGH

Covering the costs of a new product or service

THE JARGON DRAGON

capital – money invested in a business

start-up costs – costs involved in setting up a new business activity

market research – investigation into consumer likes and dislikes

running costs – the day-to-day costs of running a business

All businesses need to raise money, sometimes referred to as <u>capital</u>, for their activities. This is particularly important when the business is considering expansion. <u>Start-up costs</u> are the costs that are linked to new activities. A new business will have start-up costs but so will an established business that is trying to expand by selling new products or services.

Start-up costs include payment for <u>market research</u>, buying or expanding premises and purchasing new machinery – for example, Boots wished to launch a range of eye-care products aimed at teenagers and hired a well-known designer to research what teenagers wanted. Fixtures and fittings such as office furniture, shelving and storage cabinets are also included in start-up costs.

The expenses for day-to-day activities are called <u>running costs</u> or operating costs. Running costs include the costs of advertising, continuing market research, rent on premises, electricity to run the equipment, taxes, staff wages and the materials used in the process of production. An unusual example of running costs is the money that BMW has paid to have its cars used in certain James Bond films such as *Tomorrow Never Dies* and *The World is not Enough* to bring them to the attention of the public.

Businesses can raise finance to meet their costs in several ways (see page 174).

Promoting products is a typical running cost – this BMW Z8 is similar to one featured in the James Bond film *The World is Not Enough*

Market research in BP

case study

During 2000 BP started a world-wide market research programme about its brand in 27 countries. The purpose was to establish how the BP brand is seen. The company looked at its performance to see how it was doing by comparison with traditional competitors and other great global brands from outside the energy sector. This enabled BP to understand its brand's strengths and weaknesses and identify whether it was meeting the needs of its customers.

The programme was run by Millward Brown, a leading Market Research agency based in the UK. Interviews were conducted by telephone to establish a baseline before the launch of the new brand. In countries where BP has a retail presence they asked people for their views about our service stations. Additionally, people in all 27 countries were asked about BP as a whole – examining its business reputation and attitudes to the brand.

Based on an extract from BP's website (http://www.bpamoco.com/index.asp)

Q1 *Think of examples of costs BP would have to pay in order to carry out this work.*

Q2 *What benefits would the firm get from this sort of research?*

Q3 *Which firms might BP consider as competitors?*

Reducing running costs

Investment in information technology can help a firm reduce some of its operating costs. For example:

- Video conferencing can help reduce the expense of bringing staff together for meetings.
- E-mail can be cheaper to use than the traditional postal service.
- Computerised stock control systems in a supermarket will read the information from the barcode on packets and tins and send the information to central computers that will automatically send orders to suppliers when stocks are low. This cuts the number of administrative staff needed and can reduce wages costs or frees staff to work on other tasks.

Video conferencing reduces the need for staff to gather together in the same place

THE JARGON DRAGON

just-in-time – stock ordering system that keeps stocks low by arranging deliveries just as they are needed

For example, Coca Cola aims to keep its levels of stock as low as possible but needs to supply its 16 million customers as quickly as possible. Using computers for stock control and ordering makes sure that deliveries take place just in time for the product to be used. The **Just-in-Time** system of stock management reduces the amount of money Coca Cola has invested in stock and leaves it free to spend on other activities.

Barcodes make it easier for businesses to monitor the movement of their stock

Using a cash flow forecast

Planning the income and expenditure of a business is an important part of developing plans for the future. It is important to be able to predict what income and expenditure is likely to be needed (to monitor **cash flow**) so that the firm does not run out of funds. These predictions will help the company to make a number of decisions.

THE JARGON DRAGON

cash flow – flow of income and expenditure into and out of a business

Producing new goods or services
If we choose to develop a new product, what are the likely costs and income? How might these vary with how many items we sell?

Investing in new equipment or facilities
What income or return on investment is likely if we buy a faster, more modern machine to use in production activities? Will the new machine help reduce overall costs such as staff wages or the expense of producing faulty items?

Carrying out new activities

What income might our business gain if we invest money in the staff and equipment for some new activity, such as opening a branch in another town?

Expanding or reducing existing activities

If we combined two factories onto one site how much would we save? And how much would we have to spend to set up the new factory? Would the difference between the extra costs and the costs saved make such a change worthwhile?

Preparing a cash flow forecast

One way to make these plans and predictions is to prepare a cash flow forecast. This is simply a table showing what income and expenditure the business expects in the coming months. The cash flow forecast will show:

THE JARGON DRAGON

revenue – income into a business

- **Inflows** – income or **revenue** from sales, loans from banks, grants from government.
- **Outflows** – payments for raw materials, wages, rent, interest on loans, telephone, new machinery and taxes.

The example below covers six months, although cash flow forecasts can be prepared for any length of time.

A cash-flow forecast helps businesses plan their activities

CASH FLOW FORECAST FOR MLB PAINT MANUFACTURERS						
	April	May	June	July	August	Sept
Income						
1 Bank balance from last month	200.00	39.00	(84.00)	(175.00)	(268.00)	(236.00)
2 Sales	150.00	175.00	166.00	200.00	334.00	444.00
3 Income total	350.00	214.00	82.00	25.00	66.00	208.00
Expenditure						
4 Transport	68.00	60.00	34.00	66.00	65.00	67.00
5 Rent	20.00	20.00	20.00	20.00	20.00	20.00
6 Wages	150.00	150.00	150.00	150.00	150.00	150.00
7 Raw materials	50.00	45.00	30.00	34.00	44.00	50.00
8 Electricity	23.00	23.00	23.00	23.00	23.00	23.00
9 Expenditure total	311.00	298.00	257.00	293.00	302.00	310.00
10 End of month balance	39.00	(84.00)	(175.00)	(268.00)	(236.00)	(102.00)

Figure in brackets are overdrawn.

By looking downwards under each month we can get a picture of what money the business expects to spend and receive. We can see that Income total (line 3) is the total of lines 1 and 2. Expenditure total (line 9) is arrived at by adding together lines 4–8. Line 10 gives the end of month balance, which is line 3 minus line 9. In other words, line 10 shows the difference between income and expenditure for that month.

Figures in brackets are negative, and mean that more has gone out of the business than has come in. After having done these calculations the accountant for MLB Paint Manufacturers would advise the owners to obtain money to cover the difference in income and expenditure from June onwards. In a case like this finance might be obtained through a bank loan or a bank overdraft. In order to improve the situation shown in the figure it is clear that MLB Paint Manufacturers need to either increase sales or reduce expenditure – preferably both! Tackling the problem successfully is the responsibility of the organisation's managers. Unless sales are likely to improve or costs reduce there would be no point in this firm continuing to trade because it is not making a profit.

A cash flow forecast can also show when a firm might have extra cash coming in, which would help the owners plan to spend or invest it. A business should avoid having too much (surplus) cash as efficient businesses make sure their cash is earning income. Surplus cash could be invested in equipment, property, shares or even in a high-interest bank account.

THE JARGON DRAGON

spreadsheet   computer program used for mathematical calculations and financial records

A computer **spreadsheet** is often used to produce cash flow forecasts. This is because formulae can be entered into the spreadsheet to complete calculations as soon as numbers are put in. This is not only timesaving but also reduces the chances of errors. Most spreadsheets can produce information as graphs or charts to help readers understand the complex information.

Re-write, or type into a spreadsheet, the cash-flow forecast for MLB Paints and adjust the figures so that the business shows a surplus at the end of the period.

FIND IT OUT

So, what are accounting technicians?

Accounting technicians work in accounting and finance alongside chartered accountants, in a wide range of jobs from accounts clerks to credit control officers to financial managers. Accounting technicians work in all sectors of the economy, in industry and commerce, accountancy practices and the public and voluntary sectors. Some are self-employed, offering their services to the general public.

The Association of Accounting Technicians (AAT)

The AAT is the professional body for Accounting Technicians, with more than 100 000 members and students worldwide. Formed in 1980, it is sponsored by four of the major accountancy bodies in the UK:

- The Chartered Institute of Public Finance and Accountancy (CIPFA)

- The Institute of Chartered Accountants in England and Wales (ICAEW)

- The Chartered Institute of Management Accountants (CIMA)

- The Institute of Chartered Accountants of Scotland (ICAS).

These organisations provide non-financial support, offer fast-track entry or exemptions into their qualifications to AAT-qualified students, and are represented on the AAT's council.

The AAT is unique in that it is the only professional accounting body to be accredited by the Qualifications and Curriculum Authority (QCA), and is the only specialist awarding body for National Vocational Qualifications (NVQs) in Accounting. The AAT is also approved by the Scottish Qualifications Authority to provide Scottish Vocational Qualifications (SVQs) in Accounting.

Adapted from the AAT website http://www.aat.co.uk/index.html

Q1 *Name four types of accountants.*

Q2 *How is the AAT unique?*

Q3 *Where might you find accounting technicians working and what sort of jobs might they be doing?*

So, what are accounting technicians?

case study

Using a budget

Departments or sections of firms are often provided with money to perform their various tasks during the financial year and are set targets of how much they have to earn. These allocations and targets together are called a <u>budget</u>. By putting together the budgets for each part of the business the owners can see what the business budget for the year will look like. Budgets can be set for shorter or longer periods than this, but a year is the most common.

THE JARGON DRAGON

budget – planned income and expenditure

The management accountant

The management accountant records the activities of the business and advises managers about how well departments are doing in meeting their budgets. This allows them to make decisions, for example, to increase the department's income. Using the budget properly can help a business to plan its expenditure and check its performance.

There are different sorts of accountants in business, who are often supported by accounting technicians who carry out a number of important tasks.

Think IT THROUGH

Draw up a budget for yourself showing your income and expenditure over the course of a month. What spending would you reduce if you wanted to increase your savings?

?

Calculating the break-even point

THE JARGON DRAGON

break even – the point where total cost equals total revenue

A firm is said to **break even** when its costs are the same as its revenue. If costs are greater than revenue it is operating at a loss, if costs are lower than revenue it is operating at a profit. In order to make accurate forecasts and understand the firm's finances more fully we can break down costs and revenues into several types.

Costs

Fixed costs

These costs stay the same, regardless of the level of output (e.g. rent will be the same whether a firm produces 10 cakes or 1000 cakes, the interest on a loan to buy equipment will be the same regardless of how many items a piece of equipment produces). Fixed costs are sometimes called indirect costs. This term is used as they have to be met whether production takes place or not and so they are only indirectly related to levels of production.

Variable costs

The variable costs do change with the level of production. For example, if a firm increases production to 1000 cakes it will need to buy extra flour to make the cakes and employ more staff, which will increase the cost of wages. As a result of being directly linked to production levels these costs are sometimes called **direct costs**.

Total costs

Some costs are hard to classify. Administration costs will rise as output rises but these will not be as closely linked to output levels as the costs of raw materials. When variable cost is added to fixed costs it gives total cost. Total costs can be thought of as a line with fixed and variable costs at opposite ends. Individual costs can be placed at some point on this line near to the fixed cost end or the variable cost end, depending on what they are.

Some costs change more quickly than others as short-term changes in production occur. The costs that change most quickly are called variable costs. Fixed costs change much more slowly, if at all, in relation to productive activity

Rent   Interest rates   Labour costs, raw materials

Unit costs

Once a firm has started production an important decision is to decide what the most profitable level of output is.

The firm can only decide how many more, or fewer, items to produce if it can find out the cost of producing one item. The cost of producing one item is called **unit cost** or **average cost**. Unit cost is arrived at by dividing the total cost of production by the number of items produced. For example, if a firm makes 80

THE JARGON DRAGON

unit cost – the cost of producing one item

rubber ducks a week and total costs are £160 then the unit cost is £2.00 (i.e. 160/80).

Unit costs do not remain constant. As output increases each extra item produced has to cover less of the fixed costs, because the fixed costs are being spread over an increasing number of items. Each item as a result has a smaller share of the fixed cost to carry. Notice that each item has to share the extra variable costs needed to produce it. The table below demonstrates this point.

Increases in production can reduce unit costs, if fixed costs remain unchanged

Tins of paint produced	Fixed costs (£)	Variable costs (£)	Total costs (£)	Unit costs (£)
0	500	0.00	500	
1	500	1.00	501	501.00
10	500	10.00	510	51.00
50	500	50.00	550	11.00
150	500	150.00	650	4.33
600	500	600.00	1100	1.83
1000	500	1000.00	1500	1.50

The figures used in this example can also be shown as graphs.

The table and graphs demonstrate that even though total cost is increasing unit cost is reducing.

Change in unit cost relative to number of units produced

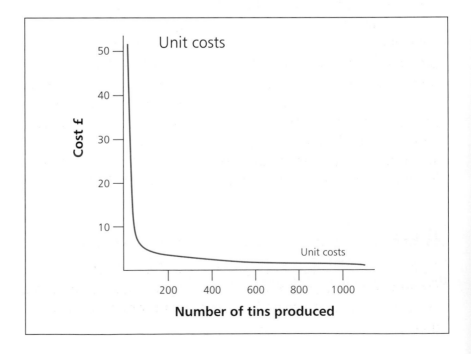

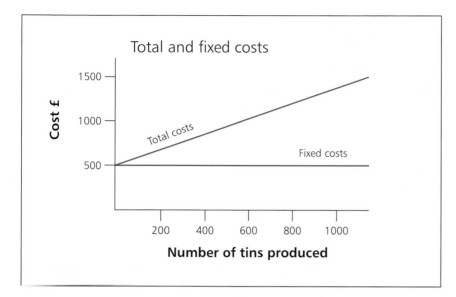

Total and fixed costs relative to the number of units produced

Cost savings

Cost savings as a result of large-scale production are called economies of scale. Economies of scale occur in advertising the firm's products. This is because as more is produced each item has to cover less of the advertising costs. The same applies to the costs of the firm's administration. The larger the size or scale of production the greater is the scope for savings or economies. Page 162 shows how economies of scale can develop as output increases.

The aim of business is to be as efficient or productive as possible. This can be done by increasing output but holding total costs steady or by producing the same amount for less cost. New technology in production and administration can make firms more productive. Halfords, for example, have used new technology to transfer all their existing data about products onto the computers of new stores. In the past this information would have to have been inputted manually. Boots Opticians has improved its store administration by introducing computerised store administration systems, which are faster than the old system and provide more information to staff so they can serve customers better.

Revenue

Revenue is the money coming into a firm. The bulk of an organisation's revenue comes from selling its products or services. Other revenue might come from investments or government grants.

Boots Opticians contributes to the
total revenue of Boots the Chemist

- Total revenue is the total income of an organisation.
  Cadbury Schweppes, for example, has a total annual
  revenue of over £4 billion.
- Average revenue is the revenue a firm receives from each
  item it sells. Average revenue is calculated by dividing total
  revenue by the number of items sold – e.g. if total revenue
  is £1400 and the firm sells 700 items average revenue is
  £2.00. We can represent revenue as a graph.

Total revenue and average revenue
against output per week

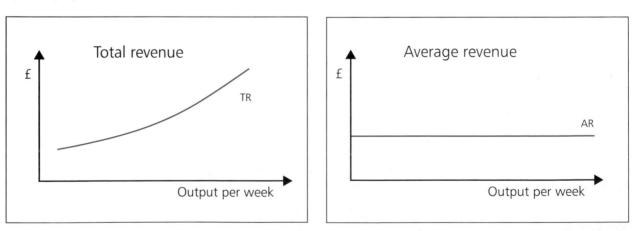

Average revenue is usually the same as the price of the item sold,
but not if a supplier sells goods at different prices to different
customers. For example, customers buying in bulk might be

quoted a lower price than customers buying only small
quantities. In this case average revenue will be different from the
price each customer pays for each item.

Breaking even

When a firm's costs balance its revenue it has broken even. If
costs are higher than revenue it is operating at a loss, and if costs
are lower than revenue it is operating at a profit. Break-even
analysis is used to show how different levels of output can affect
profits. It can also show how changes in price will affect profits
at different levels of output. The break-even charts below use
both total and average costs and revenues.

Break-even charts

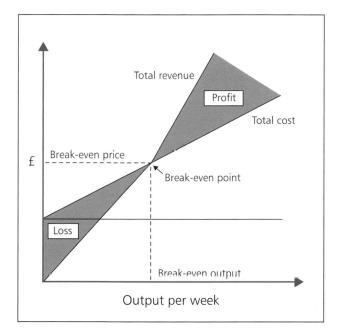

The chart shows what the firm needs to produce in order
to reach break-even point, and the price it needs to sell at.
The level of output where cost equals revenue is called the
break-even point. Notice that at all levels of output fixed costs
are the same. However, if existing capital equipment was
working at full output and more equipment was bought the
fixed cost line would rise by the amount the extra equipment
cost.

Break-even analysis is a useful tool for analysing the effects of
price changes on profit levels and for planning output levels.

The break-even point can be found using a simple calculation:

$$\text{Break even} = \frac{\text{Fixed cost}}{(\text{Selling price per unit} - \text{variable cost per unit})}$$

For example, if fixed cost = £100, selling price = £5 and variable cost = £3,

$$\text{Break even} = \frac{£100}{(£5 - £3)}$$

$$= \frac{£100}{£2}$$

$$= 50$$

In this case 50 units would need to be sold in order to break even.

Business finance is about understanding the flow of money into and out of a business

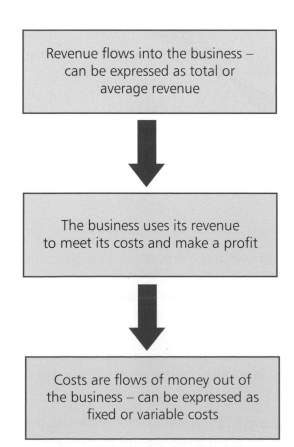

Revenue flows into the business – can be expressed as total or average revenue

The business uses its revenue to meet its costs and make a profit

Costs are flows of money out of the business – can be expressed as fixed or variable costs

Calculating the profit and loss of a business

Break-even analysis is one way of forecasting the level of profit earned by a business. Another way is to use a profit and loss account. This document shows:

- value of sales
- cost of sales
- gross **profit**
- overheads/expenses
- net profit.

THE JARGON DRAGON

profit – the amount of money remaining after all costs have been met

The profit and loss account

The profit and loss account is a summary of the total of the business's purchases and sales over a given period. It shows *net profit* – the profit left after all payments have been made. The given period is normally one year. The layout of a profit and loss account can vary but the example below demonstrates the main points.

Trading, profit and loss account for Jamie B Music Store		
A **Trading Account**		
1 Value of sales	50 000.00	
2 Staff wages		−20 000.00
3 Other expenses:		
Music and instruments		−5 000.00
Heating		−2 000.00
Rent		−2 000.00
Insurance		−1 000.00
4 *Gross profit*	*20 000.00*	
5 Gross profit	+20 000.00	
6 Income from garage rental	+5000.00	
7 Depreciation of sound system in shop		−250.00
8 Telephone bill		−5000.00
9 *Net profit (before tax)*	*+19 750.00*	
B **Appropriation Account**		
10 Net profit (before tax)	+19 750.00	
11 Taxation		−6000.00
12 Drawings		−10 000.00
13 *Balance: Net profit (after tax)*	*+3750.00*	

A profit and loss account shows how profitable a business is

As you can see, the account for this sole trader is in two parts. The trading account (Part A) shows the total value of sales for the year (line 1). Line 2 shows the total wages cost that is directly related to the running of the shop. Line 3 shows the costs of the main raw materials needed to run the shop. The trading account shows the difference between the value of sales and the costs directly related to providing the goods or services of the firm. This figure (line 4) is the *gross* profit.

Lines 5–9 take the gross profit and add any income not directly related to production (line 6). We must then remove from the figure any costs not directly related to production. In this example there is a telephone bill (line 8) and **depreciation** of equipment.

In this example the sound system is worth about £250 less now than when it was new. In other words, if it was sold now (the end of the year) Jamie would get £250 less than he would have by selling it at the start of the year. The money for depreciation is set aside so that when equipment wears out the firm is able to replace it.

The appropriation account (Part B) shows what remains when taxes, such as VAT, have been paid and **drawings** taken into account. These drawings are in addition to any wage Jamie may pay himself. Once this calculation is done we are left with the *net* profit figure (line 13). Net profit is the amount remaining after all deductions have been accounted for. The net profit is kept by the owners.

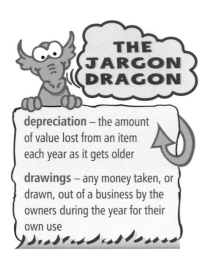

THE JARGON DRAGON

depreciation – the amount of value lost from an item each year as it gets older

drawings – any money taken, or drawn, out of a business by the owners during the year for their own use

Understanding a balance sheet

While the profit and loss account shows a summary of the firm's activities over a period of time, the balance sheet shows the value of the business on a particular day (it is rather like a putting a DVD on 'freeze' to see one frame rather than the whole film, as it looks at the firm on one day rather than looking at all of it activities). While the value of some things can be exactly calculated others have to be estimated. Despite this element of 'guesswork' the balance sheet is an important document for showing the value of business. The balance sheet is normally produced once a year and shows the result of using the firm's funds during that year. The balance sheet must contain the following details.

Share capital and reserves

The value of share capital, reserves and balance from the profit and loss account.

Current liabilities

The amount of money owed to trade creditors, interest to debenture holders, bank overdrafts and share dividend payments.

Current assets

The value of stock, work in progress (or 'in hand'), cash in the bank, cash in hand and debtors. Debtors, the people who owe the firm money, are classed as assets because they will, eventually pay money to the firm. Any debt repayments a firm gives up on are classified as bad debts. Current assets can be turned into cash quickly.

Fixed assets

Fixed assets include the value of land, premises, office equipment, motor vehicles, manufacturing equipment (or plant) and investments. Notice that for some fixed assets, such as plant, there has to be an allowance for depreciation. Fixed assets are the items that can be turned into cash, but not as quickly as current assets.

Liabilities and provisions

These include income tax, corporation tax and the cost of repaying debentures and bank loans. Businesses must set aside money to meet their liabilities.

THE JARGON DRAGON

liabilities – the debts a business has, or expects to have

Work in groups. Using the Internet or details from the Financial Times *newspaper, obtain the annual reports from two companies. Decide which company would be the best investment choice.*

FIND IT OUT

The balance sheet is important in showing the financial health of a business

Dixons Group plc   ANNUAL REPORT AND ACCOUNTS 2000/01

BALANCE SHEETS

| | | Group | | Company | |
	Note	28 April 2001 £million	29 April 2000 £million	28 April 2001 £million	29 April 2000 £million
Fixed assets					
Intangible assets	13	432.7	443.3	–	–
Tangible assets	14	535.0	501.0	0.3	0.2
Investments	15	625.7	85.8	1,775.0	1,750.2
		1,593.4	1,030.1	1,775.3	1,750.4
Current assets					
Stocks	18	580.7	512.5	–	–
Debtors	19	383.9	358.3	156.7	153.7
Investments	20	793.0	788.8	–	–
Cash at bank and in hand		64.4	103.9	9.8	1.7
		1,822.0	1,763.5	166.5	155.4
Creditors – due within one year					
Borrowing	21	(195.8)	(68.8)	–	(40.2)
Other creditors	21	(929.7)	(878.4)	(1,058.7)	(892.5)
		(1,125.5)	(947.2)	(1,058.7)	(932.7)
Net current assets/(liabilities)		696.5	816.3	(892.2)	(777.3)
Total assets less current liabilities		2,289.9	1,846.4	883.1	973.1
Creditors – due after more than one year					
Borrowing	22	(462.1)	(556.9)	–	–
Other creditors	22	(264.9)	(233.8)	–	–
		(727.0)	(790.7)	–	–
Provisions for liabilities and charges	28	(39.0)	(36.5)	(5.8)	–
		1,523.9	1,019.2	877.3	973.1
Share capital	29	48.2	47.7	48.2	47.7
Share premium account	29	94.4	50.2	94.4	50.2
Capital reserve	29	395.5	121.2	–	–
Merger reserve	29	(386.1)	(386.1)	–	–
Capital reduction reserve	29	425.5	425.5	425.5	425.5
Profit and loss account	29	917.5	718.5	309.2	449.7
Equity shareholders' funds	29	1,495.0	977.0	877.3	973.1
Equity minority interests		28.9	42.2	–	–
		1,523.9	1,019.2	877.3	973.1

The financial statements were approved by the Board of Directors on 4 July 2001 and signed on its behalf by:

Sir Stanley Kalms

Sir Stanley Kalms

Ian Livingston

Ian Livingston

Dixons Group plc
45 Annual Report & Accounts 2000/01

The importance of business accounts

Business accounts are important to the people who are affected by the business, such as

- shareholders
- managers
- employees
- bank
- customers.

These people are known as stakeholders. The profit and loss account and the balance sheet help the stakeholders understand what is happening with the business.

The managers

The managers of the business need to know how much is available to spend on stock, wages, etc. They can only do this if they know how much income is due and how much has to be paid out. When a business looks at its expected income and expenditure it is checking cash flow.

The bank

If it becomes clear that the company does not have enough money to meet its debts it might ask for a loan from a bank. In this case the bank would want to look at the company's records and would not lend money unless they gave a clear picture of the business' activity.

The shareholders

The shareholders of the business need to know if the business is making a profit or a loss. If it makes a profit they will receive a dividend, linked to how many shares they own. If it is making a loss they may decide to sell some of their shares. For example, IBM has more than 600 000 shareholders worldwide and making sure they are well informed is a major activity for the business. Many firms are developing Internet web sites to make such information available to shareholders and other stakeholders.

The government

We all pay tax to the government on our income. The Inland Revenue collects income tax on what we earn while Customs and Excise collects VAT. These organisations will want to look at the records of a business on behalf of the government to ensure the correct amounts of tax are being paid.

The customers

Accurate business accounts are needed to ensure that customers and other companies the business trades with have been treated fairly. This should make sure the business receives all that is due to it and pays other firms what they are owed.

Completing an annual return

Remember: It is a criminal offence not to deliver the company's annual return within 28 days of the made-up date, for which company secretaries and directors may be prosecuted.

What is an annual return (Form 363)?

An annual return is a snapshot of certain company information at the made-up date. It is separate from a company's annual accounts. An annual return must contain the following information:

- the name of the company
- its registered number
- the type of company it is, for example, private or public
- the registered office address of the company
- the address where certain company registers are kept if not at the registered office
- the principal business activities of the company
- the name and address of the company secretary
- the name, usual residential address, date of birth, nationality and business occupation of all the company's directors
- the date to which the annual return is made up (the made-up date).

If the company has share capital, the annual return must also contain:

- the nominal value of total issued share capital
- the names and addresses of shareholders and the number and type of shares they hold or transfer from other shareholders.

What is the made-up date?

This is the date at which all the information in an annual return must be correct. The made-up date is usually the anniversary of the incorporation of the company.

From a Companies House Leaflet on filing annual returns
(http://www.companieshouse.gov.uk)

Q1 *Why is the government so keen to receive annual returns from companies?*

Q2 *Why might stakeholders in a company be interested in a company's annual return?*

Q3 *What could happen if the annual return is not submitted on time?*

Q4 *Explain 'made-up date'.*

The employees

Employees are stakeholders who will want to know how well the business is doing. Business accounts will, for example, help them when they are negotiating pay or deciding whether to stay with the firm or apply for another job.

Sources of business finance

Owners' funds

These are commonly raised through savings. This source of finance is slow to raise the amount of money needed. The amount a person or business can save is linked to the amount earned and spent. This may mean that savings have to be made by reducing running costs. Gifts from others or an inheritance in a will also provide owners' funds.

Profits

When a business has money left over after all costs have been met, this is profit. Profits can be re-invested in the business. This is known as ploughing back the profits.

Loans

THE JARGON DRAGON

assets – items owned by a person or business

interest – a percentage added to money borrowed, in return for using the money

Most business finance is borrowed in some way. Most loans are used for short-term needs, often to buy a particular item of equipment that will, over time, earn enough to cover its own costs. Large loans can be used to cover longer term investment. In some cases a loan will have to be secured – the person borrowing the money must agree to give up some **asset**, worth at least as much as the loan, if they fail to meet the repayments. A mortgage is a particular type of secured loan. With a mortgage the asset that is secured is usually a building or piece of land that must be given up if repayments cannot be met. The borrower usually pays **interest** on the loan, a percentage the lender adds to the amount borrowed (e.g. 5%) in return for having the use of their money. The interest received is income for the lender. Interest is charged as an annual percentage rate (APR). With a loan interest is charged on the full amount from the day it is borrowed, even if the entire loan is not taken out of the bank account. This means that loans are a less flexible means of borrowing than an overdraft.

Overdrafts

An overdraft is similar to a loan and is fairly simple to arrange. It allows an individual or a business to draw more money from their bank account than is actually in it, up to an agreed limit. Interest is paid to the bank only on the amount the account is overdrawn. An overdraft gives a business flexibility in how much they draw and the amount of interest they have to pay. Overdrafts tend to be used to finance short-term needs, for instance to buy materials that the business knows it will be able to use and sell quickly.

Hire purchase

Hire purchase is a rather expensive way of finding finance to purchase equipment. It is used mainly by small firms that are not able to find alternative methods of making a purchase. Using hire purchase allows a firm immediate use of equipment that it might otherwise have to save for. When a firm wishes to purchase equipment by hire purchase it signs a hire purchase agreement with a finance house (an organisation that makes profits by providing the money the firm needs to buy the item).

Hire purchase may prove an expensive way of buying something

The finance house pays, in full, for the item. It now owns the item but allows the firm that has signed the hire purchase agreement to use it, in return for regular payments that cover the cost of the item plus interest. At the end of the agreed period the finance house hands ownership of the equipment to the firm that has made the payments. Cars, computers and photocopiers are sometimes bought on hire purchase.

Leasing

There are two sorts of leasing arrangement: operating lease and finance lease.

case study

Staples Group

Established in 1886, Huddersfield-based Staples Group is a major paper converter and polythene extruder. Staples supplies the textile industry and exports to 42 countries, but has recently developed to include the car industry.

Chairman Robert Staples believes planned investment is the best route to competitive advantage. In the last few years, the group has spent hundreds of thousands of pounds buying new machinery and acquiring other companies. 'We have recently installed two new paper converting machines at a cost of £150 000 each,' he says. 'We've also spent £60 000 on equipment for our shoulder pad manufacturing facility. This helps us to make our products more quickly and better serve customers.'

Staples tries not to borrow money, preferring to use its retained profits as a source of funds. This does, Robert accepts, mean that a quick return on his investment is important, though he sees advantages in this: 'Today, it's very difficult to plan for the long-term. You choose projects which offer a quick payback wherever possible:

it's not short-termism, because faster returns give you more money for reinvestment in other projects.' Markets are changing so quickly, he argues, that long-term schemes are more risky. Staples also says he looks closely at the likely profits when assessing future investment.

Based on an article in *From Money & Machines: A Guide to Successful Capital Investment in Manufacturing*, **DTI** (http://www.dti.gov.uk/mbp)

Q1 *Why does Mr Staples think long-term schemes are risky?*

Q2 *Which source of finance does Mr Staples prefer?*

Q3 *What sort of things would Mr Staples have to consider before he purchased the paper-converting machines?*

Operating lease

With an operating lease a firm has use of equipment but does not own it. The equipment is owned by the leasing firm. This arrangement avoids the firm using the equipment (the lessee) having to make a large payment – it can pay in small amounts over the period of the lease. By knowing how much it will have to pay over a period of time the firm can estimate the real value of the equipment by judging what it contributes to the business in relation to what it costs. Staged payments help the firm to plan its finances accurately. With an operating lease the leasing company is usually responsible for maintaining the equipment, which saves the lessee cost and inconvenience. Leasing allows the lessee to use its **capital** for other things that may earn money.

THE JARGON DRAGON

capital – money invested in a business

As technology changes and equipment becomes more advanced firms can keep up to date and abreast of competitors by leasing modern equipment without the worry and expense of a major investment. At the end of the lease period the firm either returns the equipment to the leasing company or renews the lease. At this stage they might wish to lease different, more modern equipment.

Finance lease

A finance lease is similar to hire purchase. The lessee has the opportunity to purchase the equipment at the end of the lease period.

Selling assets

By selling something that it owns (e.g. equipment, buildings or land) a firm can raise capital. This is quite a quick and simple way of raising funds. The disadvantage of selling assets is that the firm loses the use of the asset forever. Sainsbury, for example, sold its Homebase chain of stores for £17 million. This left it free to invest the income as it wished.

Government grants

The government or the European Union provide financial help to businesses in some areas of the country, in an effort to overcome problems of unemployment. Government grants do not normally have to be repaid and owners retain full control of their business. However, the process for obtaining such grants may be quite complex and time consuming.

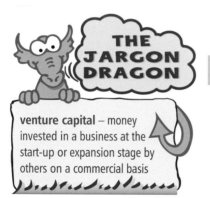

THE JARGON DRAGON

venture capital – money invested in a business at the start-up or expansion stage by others on a commercial basis

Many businesses can get help from venture capital

Venture capital

There are over 100 businesses in the UK who make money by providing **venture capital** for other businesses. In return for their investment they become part owners of the business and receive interest on the money they have loaned. Businesses can often obtain venture capital in situations that their bank might consider

as too high risk for a loan, but the owners have to share ownership and future profits with others. Businesses that have benefited from venture capital include National Express Group PLC, ABC Cinemas and Golden Wonder. These businesses used the money to purchase equipment and land to develop further.

Shares and debentures

A PLC (public limited company) can sell shares and debentures to the public. A private limited company is more restricted in who it can appeal to when selling shares or debentures.

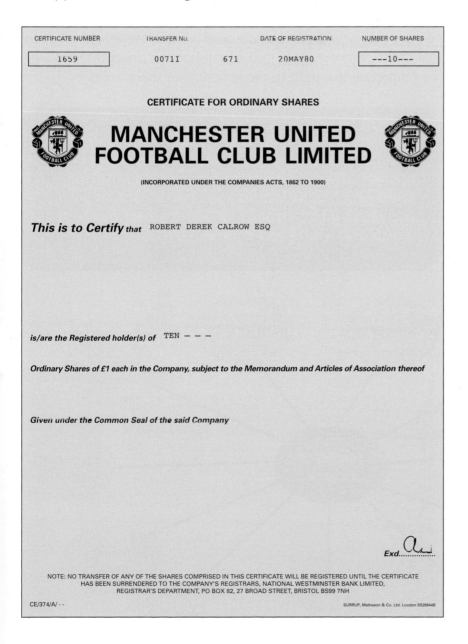

Shareholders receive a certificate as proof of their investment

Shares

Public or private limited companies can raise money by selling shares in the business. A shareholder receives a share certificate and becomes a part owner of the company. In return for their investment they receive a share of the profits, called a dividend. The company will issue different types of shares to appeal to different types of investors. Each type of share has a different level of risk attached and brings different benefits and voting rights to the shareholder.

Debentures

Debentures are loans to a company. Debenture holders are not owners of the company, but are paid a fixed rate of interest each year. If the company goes into liquidation the debenture holders have a preferential right to repayment over shareholders.

FIND IT OUT

Compare the facilities that two different banks offer for overdrafts, loans and support for business. If you wanted to have an overdraft of £800 which bank would you choose, and why? If you needed to borrow £17 000 for your business which one would you choose? Why?

There are many sources of finance available to a business

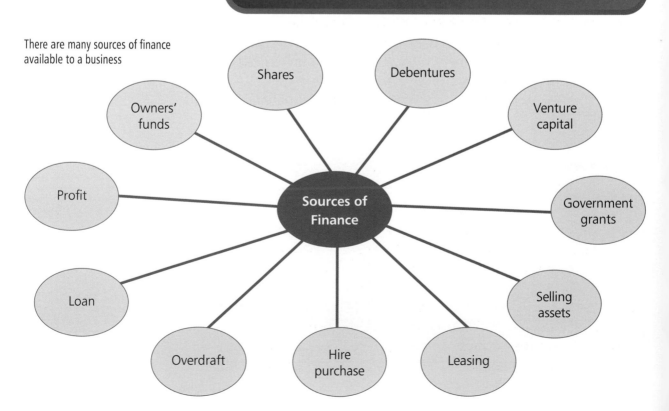

Financial planning

Financial planning is an essential activity. It affects everyone who has an interest in the business.

The business as a whole needs to plan in order to get the best use of its resources. Future activities should be planned as far ahead as possible – at the very least 12 months. By analysing the profit and loss statement, the balance sheet and other financial accounts the business' owners and managers can start to make decisions about future activities. The cash flow forecast is used to project how cash might flow in and out of the business in the next trading period. These plans, which take into consideration the wider economic and political situation, are the best judgements that can be made about future activity. They are important to the stakeholders in the business.

Investors

Investors are people who provide the business money in the hope of a making a profit when they are paid back. Anyone investing in a business will want to know about the future plans of the business to help them decide whether to continue their investment or move their money to more profitable activities. They will examine a company's published accounts and reports before they make this decision. The Internet web sites of companies are important sources of this sort of information.

Creditors

Creditors are people who lend money to the business or supply goods on credit. They make a judgement about the chances of being paid back as promised, using the financial plans of the business to help them. If a company has PLC or Ltd after its name any creditors might not be paid in full if it goes out of business. If the value of the business and its assets is less than the amount it owes creditors can not claim any more money from the shareholders of the business. If the firm is seen as a risk interest rates might be increased on any future loans – or a loan might be refused.

Looking at previous performance will help an investor decide about the future prospects of a business

CONSOLIDATED PROFIT AND LOSS ACCOUNT

	Note	52 weeks ended 28 April 2001				52 weeks ended 29 April 2000			
		Before Freeserve – continuing		Freeserve – discontinued	Total	Before Freeserve – continuing		Freeserve – discontinued	Total
		Underlying results £million	Exceptional items £million	£million	£million	Underlying results £million	Exceptional items £million	£million	£million
Turnover	2,3	4,643.4	–	44.8	4,688.2	3,871.9	–	18.0	3,889.9
Operating profit before exceptional items		282.0		(33.1)	248.9	242.2		(20.4)	221.8
Exceptional operating items	4	–	(39.3)	(0.4)	(39.7)	–	(4.9)	–	(4.9)
Group operating profit		282.0	(39.3)	(33.5)	209.2	242.2	(4.9)	(20.4)	216.9
Share of loss of associates		–	–	(5.4)	(5.4)	–	–	(2.7)	(2.7)
Total operating profit	2,3	282.0	(39.3)	(38.9)	203.8	242.2	(4.9)	(23.1)	214.2
Exceptional items	4	–	471.8	–	471.8	–	236.2	(1.9)	234.3
Profit on ordinary activities before interest		282.0	432.5	(38.9)	675.6	242.2	231.3	(25.0)	448.5
Net interest	5	(4.2)	–	2.2	(2.0)	21.5	–	3.4	24.9
Amounts written off investments		–	(15.0)	(11.5)	(26.5)	–	–	(1.3)	(1.3)
Profit on ordinary activities before taxation		277.8	417.5	(48.2)	647.1	263.7	231.3	(22.9)	472.1
Taxation on profit on ordinary activities	10	(57.8)	8.8	7.0	(42.0)	(59.1)	0.7	4.3	(54.1)
Profit on ordinary activities after taxation		220.0	426.3	(41.2)	605.1	204.6	232.0	(18.6)	418.0
Equity minority interests					(2.5)				(4.3)
Profit for the period					602.6				413.7
Dividends – Preference	11				–				(2.2)
– Ordinary	11				(105.9)				(124.3)
Retained profit for the period					496.7				287.2
Earnings per ordinary share (pence)	12								
Adjusted diluted (before exceptional items and Freeserve)					10.7p				10.1p
Basic					31.5p				22.5p
Diluted					31.0p				21.1p

Freeserve plc was sold on 13 February 2001 and is therefore treated as a discontinued operation. All other turnover and operating profit are derived from continuing operations.

STATEMENT OF TOTAL RECOGNISED GAINS AND LOSSES

	52 weeks ended 28 April 2001 £million	52 weeks ended 29 April 2000 £million
Profit for the period	602.6	413.7
Translation adjustments	0.9	(2.6)
Total gains and losses recognised in the period	603.5	411.1

Dixons Group plc
44 Annual Report & Accounts 2000/01

Departments within a business

The separate departments within a firm will be allocated a budget to operate with at the start of each year. They will use the financial plans of the business to organise their own activities to help them meet these plans – by setting their own income or sales targets, perhaps. For example, if the business plans expect sales to rise by 10% the personnel department might have to work with the sales department to recruit extra staff to help achieve that target.

Keeping financial records

Accurate and up-to-date financial records are important in developing business plans. Owners and managers can use computer spreadsheets to calculate the costs to the business of expanding and the income from expanding. They can also use the computer to calculate the cost of unexpected events. For example, the loss of income caused by closing a branch of a chain of stores because of flooding can be calculated against the ongoing costs of the business. This would allow plans and activities at other branches to be adjusted to deal with the situation. The impact on a firm's profits of increases or decreases in costs of raw materials can be calculated, and a decision made to invest more or less to invest in the future.

If you had £3000 to invest in a local business which one would you choose? Why?

Think
IT THROUGH

Glossary

Accountant	Person who keeps financial records
Agenda	List of items to be discussed at a meeting
Aims	A list of things that a business wants to achieve (e.g. making a profit, being environmentally friendly)
Applicant	Person applying for a job
Assets	Items owned by a person or business
Assisted areas	Parts of the country with high unemployment where government help is available to businesses
Average cost	Total cost of production divided by number of items produced
Benefits	Rewards, other than pay, received by an employee
Bonus	Additional payment for meeting certain business requirements
Break even	The point where total cost equals total revenue
Budget	Planned income and expenditure
Business functions	Tasks that have to be carried out by all businesses
Business rates	Business tax paid to local council based on the estimated rental value of the business's premises
Capital	Money invested in a business
Capital goods	Goods used by businesses to make other goods and services for sale
Cash flow	Flow of income and expenditure into and out of a business
CBI	Confederation of British Industry – organisation that represents employers
Code of practice	Written guidelines on good business procedures

Collective bargaining	Negotiations about working conditions between representatives of employers and representatives of unions
Commission	Payment that is related to the value of sales made
Computer-aided design (CAD)	Designing on a computer screen using software design packages
Computer-aided manufacture (CAM)	Allows computers to operate parts of the manufacturing process
Constructive dismissal	Unreasonable actions forcing an employee to leave their job
Consumer goods	Goods sold to individuals for their own use
Contract of employment	Legal agreement describing terms of employment
Core time	Set working hours within flexitime arrangements
Cost-effective	Activity that has desired results at a reasonable cost
Council of Ministers	Group of politicians from member countries of the European Union who represent their country's views
Council tax	Household tax paid to local council based on the value of your house
Credit	Providing a product or service to a customer and being paid sometime afterwards
Credit check	When a seller makes sure a purchaser is able to pay for items purchased
Creditor	Person who lends money to the business or supplies goods on credit
Data	Items of information
Debit card	Card that removes money from purchaser's account when sale is made, unlike a credit card, which allows time to pay
Democratic	Method of organisation where members have a say in how things are organised. This is usually done through members voting for elected representatives

Depreciation	The amount of value lost from an item each year as it gets older
Direct costs	See variable costs
Dismissal	Employee is required to leave their job
Drawings	Any money taken, or drawn out of a business by the owners during the year for their own use
EFTPOS	Electronic method of collecting payment
Enterprise Grant	Financial help from government to businesses in Assisted Areas
EU	The European Union – a group of European Countries who act together to improve trade and develop closer working relations
Euro	Currency shared by several countries in the European Union, represented by the symbol €
Exchange rate	How much of one currency can be exchanged for another
Fixed costs	Costs that do not change as production levels change (e.g. rent)
Flexitime	An arrangement of flexible working hours
Franchise	An agreement for one business to copy the successful organisation of another
Franchisee	Someone who buys a franchise
Franchisor	The firm that sells a franchise business to a franchisee
Fringe benefits	Non-pay rewards to employees (e.g. company car)
Goods	Physical objects that can be transferred to others
Gross misconduct	Dishonesty, theft, fighting and drunkenness, which may be grounds for immediate dismissal
Headed paper	Paper with pre-printed business details used for writing letters

Indirect costs	*See* Fixed costs
Induction training	Training given at the start of a new job to show how the activities of the firm are organised
Industrial relations	System of negotiation between employers and employees
Interest	A percentage added to money borrowed, in return for using the money
Intranet	Run by companies and organisations as a private network for the benefit of their own staff
Investor	Person who provides money for the business, hoping to make a profit
Jargon	Specialist terms or phrases used in a particular industry (e.g. computing or nursing)
Job description	A document listing all the tasks required to be done by someone in this post
Job rotation	Workers regularly swap jobs with other people in their section
Just-in-time	Stock ordering system that keeps stocks low by arranging deliveries just as they are needed
Liabilities	Money that a business owes to others
Limited liability	Responsibility for debts limited to the amount invested
Market research	Investigation into consumer likes and dislikes
Market share	The percentage of possible customers who actually buy one particular firm's product
Maximise sales	Sell as many as possible
Merchantable quality	Goods must be of the standard expected of similar goods purchased in the same way
Misconduct	Any behaviour that is disruptive or results in poor job performance

New Deal	Government scheme to help unemployed people retrain and gain work experience
Notice of meeting	A memo containing details of time, place and date of a meeting
Notice period	The period of time an employee must work before leaving their job
Objectives	The targets a business sets itself to check it is going to achieve its aims
Ongoing training	Training to develop new skills, given either at work or outside
Online	Working through the Internet
Overtime	Hours worked over and above the normal working week, normally paid at a higher hourly rate
PAYE	Pay As You Earn – method of paying tax in instalments, based on the previous year's income and personal circumstances
Payment in lieu of notice	Employee is paid for the notice period but not required to work
Personality assessment	Psychological test to assess whether a person is suitable for a particular job
Person specification	Information on the skills, qualifications and experience a person needs to do a particular job well
Piece rate	Payment based on a worker's output
PO box	Post Office box, where a firm's mail is delivered and stored ready for collection
Premises	Place where business is carried out
Premium product	High status product that can be sold for a high price
Pressure group	Organisation that attempts to influence government and public opinion on a particular issue
Primary data	Data from market research directly related to a new product
Product life cycle	Pattern of sales after launching a new product

Productivity	The amount produced using a particular level of resources
Profit	The amount of money remaining after all costs have been met
Raw goods	Objects taken from nature (e.g. timber and coal)
Raw materials	*See* Raw goods
Redundant	Employee is no longer required to work
Referee	Person who describes an applicant to a potential employer
Reference	Information written about a person concerning their skills and proficiency
Remittance	Payment and details
Retail	Shop open to the public
Return	Money received as a result of making an investment
Revenue	Income into a business
Running costs	Day-to-day costs of running a business
Sales revenue	Money a firm receives from selling things
Secondary data	Information already collected, which is used for further market analysis
Services	Activities performed by people for others that cannot be transferred
Shareholders	Part owners of a company
Shortlist	List of potentially suitable applicants to be interviewed for a job
Sick note	Official document confirming employee illness
Software applications	Computer programs used for certain tasks, e.g. word processors or spreadsheets
Sole trader	The sole owner of a business, also sometimes called sole proprietor
Spreadsheet	Computer program used for mathematical calculations and financial records

Staff development	Training and helping staff to improve in their jobs
Stakeholder	Person who is affected by the actions of a business
Start-up costs	Costs involved in setting up a new business activity
Strike	Refusal of employees to work, as part of a dispute with an employer
Terms of reference	A list in a report of what an individual or group has been asked to do
Test market	Selling and advertising a new product in a small area to test market reaction
Time rate	Pay is based on a fixed fee per hour
Transaction	The act of buying or selling
TUC	The Trades Union Congress – an organisation that represents trade unions
UNISON	A large trade union
Unit cost	The cost of producing one item
Unlimited liability	Responsible for unlimited amount of business debt
Unsocial hours	Hours worked outside the normal office hours
Variable costs	Those costs which change as production levels change (e.g. raw materials)
VAT	Value Added Tax – a tax on purchases
Venture capital	Money invested in a business at the start-up or expansion stage by others on a commercial basis
Wholesale	Selling large quantities to shops from large warehouses

Index